IN/SPECTRE

W9-CPP-857

10

CONTENTS

CHAPTER 23: "RIKKA RETURNS"

シャー
SISSS
CRACKLE
パチ
CRACKLE
パチ
CRACKLE
パチ
YOU STILL HAVEN'T MANAGED TO FIND RIKKA-SAN?
FSHHH
しゅ~…
I DO GET THE OCCASIONAL EYE-WITNESS REPORT, BUT NEVER ANYTHING DEFINITIVE ENOUGH TO PINPOINT A LOCATION.

WE'RE ALREADY HALFWAY THROUGH JULY.

IT'S BEEN ALMOST A YEAR SINCE SHE DISAPPEARED.

STLISH

I'VE INSTRUCTED ALL OF THE YÔKAI AND AYAKASHI IN THE COUNTRY TO NOTIFY ME IF THEY SEE HER.

BUT EVEN IF THEY DO FIND HER, THAT DOESN'T MEAN I'LL GET THE REPORT IN A TIMELY MANNER.

YOU AND RIKKA-SAN WERE RELATIVELY CLOSE, WEREN'T YOU?

I REMEMBER A CONVERSATION WE HAD WHEN SHE WAS STAYING AT THE MANOR WITH ME.

KOTOKO-SAN.

WHAT ARE YOU AFRAID OF?

LET ME THINK. YOU COULD TRY TO SCARE ME WITH A HOT CUP OF TEA.

もぐ MUNCH

もぐ MUNCH

DON'T TELL ME YOU'VE NEVER HEARD THE RAKUGO STORY "MANJU KOWAI"?

WHAT PROBLEM COULD YOU POSSIBLY HAVE WITH MY WITTY COME-BACK?

WHAT I'M SAYING IS, WHEN SOMEONE'S ASKING YOU A SERIOUS QUESTION, DON'T TRY AND DISTRACT THEM WITH ANCIENT RAKUGO REFERENCES.

AND DON'T JUMP RIGHT TO THE PUNCHLINE.

YOU'RE SPOILING THE ENDING.

THERE ARE NO SPOILERS IN ANCIENT RAKUGO.

BESIDES, I CAN'T THINK OF ANYTHING I'M AFRAID OF.

WELL, I KNOW A LOT OF GIRLS WHO ARE SCARED OF SPIDERS.

ぱち CLACK

I HAD A CONSULTATION WITH A GIANT SPIDER THE OTHER DAY. I DIDN'T FIND ANYTHING PARTICULARLY FRIGHTENING ABOUT IT.

I MEAN, SURE, IT HAD LONG LEGS, BUT A SIMPLE FIST TO THE FACE WOULD HAVE EASILY SPLIT ITS HEAD IN TWO.

すい SWISH

SWISH すっ

THEN WHAT ABOUT SNAKES?
CLACK
パチ
THEY'RE OLD HAT.

CLACK
パチ
INSECTS?
I'M GUESSING THEY DON'T BOTHER YOU, EITHER.

IF I WERE SCARED OF BUGS, I WOULDN'T BE ABLE TO GO TO THE MOUNTAINS OR ABANDONED BUILDINGS WHERE MOST YÔKAI LIVE.

THEN ARE YOU AFRAID OF KURÔ HATING YOU?
OH, RIGHT, HE ALREADY HATES YOU.

MRRRGH.
角行
HE DOES NOT HATE ME.

AND IN ANY CASE, ANY LONG-TERM RELATIONSHIP IS GOING TO HAVE ITS UPS AND DOWNS.
IT'S NOTHING TO BE AFRAID OF.
SO I TAKE IT YOU'RE NOT SCARED THAT HE'LL DUMP YOU, EITHER.
OH, RIGHT, HE PRACTICALLY ALREADY HAS.

HE HAS NOT!
BESIDES, IF THAT DOES HAPPEN, THERE ARE ANY NUMBER OF WAYS TO RESOLVE THE ISSUE.

DON'T YOU THINK YOU'RE STARTING TO SOUND LIKE A STALKER?

HOW DARE YOU SLANDER ME LIKE THAT WHEN YOU'RE LIVING IN MY HOUSE RENT-FREE?

YOUR PARENTS LIKE ME.
AND THAT'S THE THING.
WHAT COULD MY PARENTS POSSIBLY SEE IN A SKELETON-WOMAN LIKE YOU?
AND HOW DARE YOU TALK THAT WAY ABOUT YOUR BOYFRIEND'S BELOVED COUSIN?

THE POINT IS, I KNOW THAT NOTHING GOOD WILL COME OF TELLING YOU WHAT I'M AFRAID OF.
SO, RIKKA-SAN.
WHAT ARE YOU AFRAID OF?

YOU SCARE ME MORE THAN ANY-THING.
KOTOKO-SAN.
WOW, RIKKA-SAN MUST REALLY HATE YOU.
EXCUSE ME! IF YOU WERE FOLLOWING THE WHOLE CONVERSA-TION, I *BELIEVE* THAT LAST BIT WAS AN EXPRESSION OF HER POSITIVE OPINION OF ME?

TWO MONTHS PREVIOUS, MAY 14.
SOMEWHERE IN JAPAN.

ぱく
CHOMP
もぐ
MUNCH
もぐ
MUNCH
ガチャ
KA-CHAK
カン
CLANG
カン
CLANG

HELLO, SAKURAGAWA-SAN.
OH, MR. MANAGER.
HELLO.
IS SOMETHING THE MATTER?
I FORGOT TO TAKE THE TAPE OFF OF APARTMENT 305'S MAILBOX.
YOU'VE BEEN HERE A WHOLE WEEK, TOO. I'M SORRY I DIDN'T REALIZE.
KAZUYUKI KONNO
WEB DESIGNER AND APARTMENT MANAGER
THAT'S ALL RIGHT. I NEVER GET MAIL ANYWAY.
RRRRIP
305
YEAH, BUT STILL...
THWIP
TEP
TEP
KAZUYUKI!

OH.
ARE YOU THE NEW TENANT?
YEAH.
SHE MOVED IN LAST WEEK.
BOW
RIKKA SAKURA-GAWA.
THIS IS MY GIRL-FRIEND, MARUMI OKI.
NICE TO MEET YOU.
YOUR BOYFRIEND REALLY HELPED ME OUT WHEN I MOVED IN.
HE TOLD ME WHERE I COULD BUY SOME NECESSI-TIES AND EVEN GOT HIS FRIEND TO GIVE ME SOME HAND-ME-DOWN FURNITURE.
I REALLY APPRECIATE ALL YOU DID FOR ME.
IT WAS NOTH-ING.
ARE YOU GOING SOME-WHERE?
YES.

FLUTTER
Times Horse Races Date
XX (Sat.)
Race
QUINELLA
10 - 6
¥20,000
Total: ★★ ¥20,000
OFF TO THE HORSE RACES.

Oohh!
THE HORS-ES, EH?
I WASN'T EXPECTING THAT. I HOPE YOU WIN.

SEE YOU LATER.
SHE WAS GORGEOUS.
YEAH, BUT YOU'RE THE ONLY ONE FOR ME, MARUMI.
I KNOW. SHE'S TOO THIN FOR YOUR TASTE.
BUT SHE HAD A KIND OF UNUSUAL VIBE ABOUT HER.

305
304
WAIT, KAZUYUKI.
DON'T TELL ME SHE MOVED INTO *YOU-KNOW-WHERE*...

WHAM

Z-ZSH
THUD
AAAAAH!

SAKURA-GAWA-SAN?!
BUILDING: COIN LAUNDRY
SHE—
SHE WAS TRYING TO SAVE MY LITTLE BOY!
ぶる SHIVER
ぶる SHIVER
AND SHE...
HNN!
ザッ DASH
MARUMI! CALL AN AMBU-LANCE!
O-OKAY!
SAKURA-GAWA-SAN!
ムク... MRK
DON'T WORRY ABOUT ME.
I'M FINE.
...!
Whew.

WHAT? BUT...
HUH?
BLOOD...
UM...
YOU'RE NOT HURT?!

NOT ESPE-CIALLY.
N— NOT ESPE-CIALLY?

BUT THAT'S IMPOS-SIBLE.
YOU FLEW THROUGH THE AIR, AND LANDED...

...

OH, IT'S JUST LIKE, YOU KNOW, IN THOSE HISTORICAL DRAMAS.
SOMEONE GETS HIT WITH A SWORD, BUT THEY'RE FINE.
THAT'S IT.
I WAS HIT BY THE BLUNT END.

THE BLUNT END... OF A TRUCK?!
Where would that even be?!
BLUNT END OR NOT, IT CAN STILL KILL PEOPLE!
EVEN WITHOUT A SHARP END, A JAPANESE SWORD CAN MAKE A REALLY GOOD CLUB. IT WOULDN'T TAKE MUCH FOR IT TO SPLIT A SKULL IN—
こん CHOP
こん CHOP
KAZUYUKI, THE AMBULANCE IS HERE!
GASP
ピーポー WEE-OO
ピーポー WEE-OO
ANYWAY, GO TO THE HOSPITAL!
BUT —
ド THUD
ガタン CLATTER
AWW.
OH, BOTHER.
ピーポー WEE-OO
ピーポー WEE-OO
ポー... OO
YOU SEE? IT *IS* CURSED!
THAT APARTMENT IS CURSED!

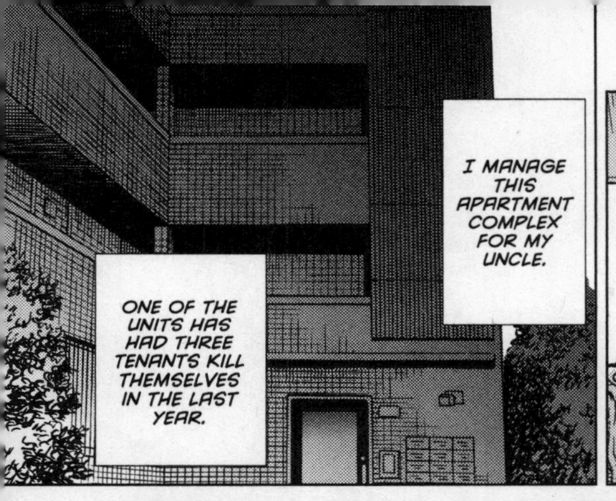
I MANAGE THIS APARTMENT COMPLEX FOR MY UNCLE.
ONE OF THE UNITS HAS HAD THREE TENANTS KILL THEMSELVES IN THE LAST YEAR.

I DUNNO, IT WAS AN ACCIDENT THIS TIME. IT COULD JUST BE A COIN-CIDENCE.

IT'S WHAT THEY CALL A STIG-MATIZED PROPERTY.
305
AN APARTMENT WITH A DARK PAST.

EVEN THE KIND OF PEOPLE WHO ACTUALLY LOOK FOR THESE PROPERTIES HAVE STARTED AVOIDING THIS ONE.
AND IT HAD BEEN VACANT FOR SOME TIME.
UNTIL SAKURAGAWA-SAN WAS APPROVED TO MOVE INTO APARTMENT 305.

IF WE GET A FOURTH VICTIM, THEN IT'LL HAVE A *REAL* STIGMA.

ANYWAY, SHOULDN'T WE TELL SAKURAGAWA-SAN'S RELATIVES ABOUT THE ACCIDENT?

WELL ...
SHE MOVED IN LAST WEEK WITH JUST ONE PIECE OF LUGGAGE—NO FURNITURE, NO APPLIANCES, NOT EVEN A BLANKET.
WHAT?

IT WAS LIKE SHE'D RUN AWAY FROM SOMEWHERE AND ONLY BROUGHT THE BARE NECESSITIES WITH HER.
I TALKED TO MY UNCLE ABOUT IT OVER THE PHONE.
HE SAID SHE DOESN'T HAVE A CO-SIGNER, AND HE COULDN'T GET IN TOUCH WITH HER FAMILY OR ANY RELATIVES.
Owner
Apartment Manager
KAZUYUKI
LIVES HERE FOR CHEAP IN EXCHANGE FOR MANAGING THE PROPERTY.
UNCLE
WON'T ANYONE MOVE INTO THIS STIGMATIZED PROPERTY? I'LL MAKE IT CHEAP, AND I DON'T CARE ABOUT YOUR PAST.
Tenant
RIKKA
I'LL TAKE IT!

WELL, I COULD TELL FROM LOOKING AT HER THAT SHE HAD A HISTORY.
AND IT'S ONLY NATURAL FOR A PERSON WITH A HISTORY TO MOVE INTO AN APARTMENT WITH A HISTORY.
BEEP

WAAH
WAAH
WITH LESS THAN 200 YARDS TO GO...
NUMBER 10, SALTED GIZZARD, TAKES THE LEAD!
STAMP
STAMP
STAMP
AND IN SECOND PLACE WE HAVE, SCALLION SKEWER HOLD THE SCALLIONS, WITH NUMBER 6, CHICKEN BREAST CARTILAGE, CLOSING IN!
Sakuragawa-san's betting ticket?
OH!
ISN'T THAT...?
YEAH. SHE DROPPED IT ON THE STREET.
Figure I can at least see how she did.
NUMBER 10 SALTED GIZZARD SIDESTEPS CHICKEN BREAST CARTILAGE AND CROSSES THE FINISH LINE!
THE WINNER IS SALTED GIZZARD!
WAAAH
WAAH
AND CHICKEN BREAST CARTILAGE TAKES SECOND!
WAAH
FOL-LOWED BY SHISO CHICKEN MEAT-BALL!
QUINELLA
10 - 6
WHOA! SHE WON!
NO WAY!
I GUESS SHE'S SMARTER ABOUT HORSE RACING THAN SHE LOOKS.
HOW MUCH DID SHE WIN?
QUINELLA 10-6
EXACTA 10-6
LET'S SEE, A QUINELLA? THE RETURN ON THAT IS 13,000 YEN.
AND SHE BET 20,000.
QUINELLA
10 - 6
Total: ★★ ¥20,000

2.6 million yen*.
WHAT?!
HUH...?
MMMM?
JOLT
NO, MAYBE I DID THE MATH WRONG.
I DON'T KNOW THAT MUCH ABOUT HORSE-RACING.
COME ON! FIND THE EXACT NUMBER!
*ABOUT $26,000

...I WAS RIGHT.
THEN THIS IS LIKE A GOLDEN TICKET?
WOW...

SO, DO YOU KNOW WHAT SAKURAGAWA-SAN DOES, OR WHY SHE CAME HERE?

SHE HASN'T TOLD ME ANY DETAILS ...

ピンポーン
DING DONG
ビクッ
WINCE
ビクーッ
WINCE

ガチャ
KA-CHAK

SA-
SAKURA-GAWA-SAN?!
I'M SORRY FOR THE TROUBLE I CAUSED THIS AFTERNOON.

BECAUSE, AS YOU CAN SEE, THERE'S NOTHING WRONG WITH ME.

WEREN'T YOU AT THE HOSPITAL?!
THEY DIS-CHARGED ME.

RUSTLE
AND I THOUGHT I'D BRING YOU THIS, AS THANKS FOR ALL YOUR HELP.
BEER

I... I SEE. ...WELL.
IN THAT CASE, I'M GLAD YOU'RE OKAY.
IT'S A MIRACLE YOU SURVIVED THAT AC-CIDENT!
WHEW

OH, IT WAS NOTHING SPECIAL.
SAKURA-GAWA-SAN!
LOOK!
IT'S A GOLDEN TICKET!
STOMP
STOMP

OH.
YOU PICKED UP MY TICKET? THANK YOU.
B-BUT YOUR WINNINGS! IT'S INCREDIBLE!
OH, IT'S NOT THAT UNCOMMON.

...
GOOD-BYE.
UM.
SAKURA-GAWA-SAN.

...GOOD POINT. IT *IS* MORE FUN TO DRINK WITH GOOD COMPANY.
SO I THINK I WILL STAY.
ぱたん
SHUT
I DID HEAR ABOUT THE THREE SUICIDES, BUT I'M NOT TOO WORRIED ABOUT IT.
ジュウ
SIZZLE
ジュウ
-SIZZLE
REALLY? THAT ACCIDENT THIS AFTERNOON PRACTICALLY GAVE ME A HEART ATTACK—WE THOUGHT YOU WERE THE FOURTH VICTIM.
IT WAS TOTALLY UNRELATED.
IT SAVED ME SOME TROUBLE, IN FACT.
?

BUT HAVE YOU EXPERIENCED ANYTHING UNUSUAL?
YOU KNOW ...
LIKE HAVE YOU HEARD THINGS GOING BUMP IN THE NIGHT, OR SEEN STRANGE SHADOWS IN THE CORNER OF YOUR EYE?
NO, NOTHING IN PARTICU-LAR.

CAN: DRAFT

SO HIS REASON FOR KILLING HIMSELF HAD NOTHING TO DO WITH THE APARTMENT ITSELF.

AND BECAUSE OF HIS SUICIDE, YOU HAD TO LOWER THE RENT ON THE UNIT,

MAKING IT MORE ACCESSIBLE TO PEOPLE WITH DARK HISTORIES.

IN THAT CASE, WOULDN'T THE SECOND PERSON HAVE HAD A REASON TO COMMIT SUICIDE, AS WELL?

YES ...

WELL ...

THE SECOND TENANT WAS A WOMAN IN HER LATE TWENTIES.
SHE HAD BEEN LIVING WITH A MAN, AND THEY WERE EVEN ENGAGED, BUT THEN HE DUMPED HER IN THE WORST WAY POSSIBLE.
AFTER THAT, SHE NEEDED A NEW JOB AND PLACE TO LIVE, SO SHE CAME HERE.

SHE MADE A FRESH START, AND WE ALL THOUGHT THINGS WERE GOING PRETTY WELL, BUT THREE MONTHS LATER, SHE KILLED HERSELF.

SHE DIDN'T LEAVE A NOTE, SO IT WAS LIKE THE SPIRIT OF THE PREVIOUS TENANT HAD TAKEN HER WITH HIM.

SO SHE ALREADY HAD A REASON TO WANT TO KILL HERSELF, AND IF SHE HAD DONE IT RIGHT AFTER THE BREAKUP, NOBODY WOULD HAVE BEEN SURPRISED.

SHE HUNG ON FOR ANOTHER THREE MONTHS, BUT SHE JUST COULDN'T RECOVER FROM THE HEARTBREAK.
ONE DAY, IT GOT TO BE TOO MUCH, AND SHE KILLED HERSELF.
IT DOESN'T SOUND LIKE ANYTHING OUT OF THE ORDINARY.
NOTHING THAT WOULD REQUIRE ANY SUPER-NATURAL OR PARANORMAL POWERS.
CLUNK
BUT THAT DOESN'T HOLD TRUE FOR THE THIRD TENANT.
HE WAS A PENCIL PUSHER, ABOUT 30 YEARS OLD, AND HE KILLED HIMSELF THREE MONTHS AFTER MOVING IN, TOO.
HE HAD A GIRL-FRIEND, AND WORK WAS GOING WELL.
THERE WAS NO OBVIOUS REASON FOR HIM TO TAKE HIS OWN LIFE.

HE DIDN'T LEAVE A NOTE, EITHER.

IT SEEMED SUSPICIOUS, SO WE HAD THE POLICE INVESTIGATE IT.

THAT'S WHEN WE LEARNED THAT HE WAS THE EX-BOYFRIEND OF THE SECOND PERSON TO KILL HERSELF IN THAT APARTMENT.

TAPE: KEEP OUT

AFTER THE SECOND SUICIDE,

RUMORS STARTED GOING AROUND THAT THE APARTMENT MIGHT BE HAUNTED.

AFTER THE THIRD SUICIDE, EVERYBODY WAS CONVINCED.

HMM...

SO WHY *DID* YOU DECIDE TO LIVE IN THAT APARTMENT, SAKURAGAWA-SAN?

I HEARD YOU WEREN'T EVEN REALLY PREPARED FOR A MOVE.

BUT IT DOESN'T SEEM LIKE YOU'RE HURTING FOR MONEY, EITHER.

SIGH
I HAVE A COUSIN, THREE YEARS YOUNGER THAN ME, AND A HORRIBLE GIRL HAS HIM IN HER EVIL CLUTCHES.
I STAYED OPTIMISTIC. I TOLD MYSELF I DIDN'T HAVE TO DO ANYTHING— HE WOULD BREAK IT OFF WITH HER BEFORE LONG.
BUT THEN IT LOOKED LIKE THEY WERE ACTUALLY GETTING CLOSER.
GULP
GULP
COUSIN...?
I COULDN'T LET IT GO ON, SO I GOT TO WORK AND TRIED TO BREAK THEM UP.
BUT SHE'S REALLY JUST SO HORRIBLE. SHE SHOWS NO SIGNS OF EVER LEAVING HIM.
UH-HUH...

IF MY COUSIN AND I COULD JUST BE NORMAL HUMAN BEINGS, HE'D BE ABLE TO BREAK TIES WITH HER COMPLETELY.
CHOMP ぱく
I'VE TRIED EVERYTHING I COULD THINK OF, BUT THIS HORRIBLE GIRL BLOCKS ME AT EVERY TURN.
もぐ MUNCH
もぐ MUNCH
ひょい YOINK
CHOMP ぱく
IN THE END, *I'M* THE ONE THAT HAD TO GO INTO HIDING.
NORMAL HUMAN BEINGS?
DON'T READ TOO MUCH INTO IT.
IT'S JUST THAT THAT GIRL IS NOT NORMAL.
THIS APARTMENT IS THE PERFECT PLACE TO SETTLE DOWN AND THINK UP MY NEXT PLAN, SO I RENTED IT AS A SORT OF TEMPORARY REFUGE.
BUT I CAN'T STAY HERE LONG. I DON'T WANT THAT GIRL FINDING ME.

?
?
I HAVEN'T DONE ANYTHING ILLEGAL, SO YOU DON'T HAVE TO WORRY ABOUT THAT.
BUT IF THINGS GO ON THIS WAY...
...THEN MY COUSIN WILL BE FORCED TO SUFFER CRUEL HEARTBREAK AND MISERY AT THE HANDS OF THIS GIRL.
HE JUST DOESN'T UNDER-STAND.
HE CAN BE VERY DIM SOME-TIMES.
I WANT TO PUT A STOP TO THIS QUICKLY, BUT...
YOU CARE VERY MUCH ABOUT THIS COUSIN OF YOURS.

HE WAS SUPPOSED TO BE MINE.

FZHHH

WHAT KIND OF A GIRL WOULD MAKE *THAT* WOMAN CALL HER HORRIBLE?

MAYBE SHE'S ACTUALLY TOUGH COMPETI-TION?

LIKE, SHE'S PRETTIER THAN SAKURAGAWA-SAN.

MORE IMPRESSIVE.

WEARS HER YOUTH LIKE A BADGE OF HONOR.

MAYBE SHE'S ARROGANT, TOO.

THAT SOUNDS TERRIFYING.

BUILDING: COIN LAUNDRY

SOUNDS LIKE SHE WAS BORN UNDER AN *UN*-LUCKY STAR, IF YOU ASK ME.
MAYBE SO.
IT'S BEEN ALMOST THREE MONTHS SINCE SAKURA-GAWA-SAN MOVED IN.
I HOPE NOTHING HAPPENS TO HER.
ピンポーン
DING DONG
ガチャ
KA-CHAK
HUH?
WHAT'S UP? IT'S THE MIDDLE OF THE NIGHT.
I APOLO-GIZE FOR THE LATE-NESS OF THE HOUR.
IT SEEMS THAT MY COUSIN AND THAT GIRL HAVE LEARNED MY WHERE-ABOUTS.
SO, I KNOW THIS IS SUDDEN, BUT YOU WON'T SEE ME AGAIN.

HUH?
I'D LIKE YOU TO DISPOSE OF EVERYTHING I LEFT IN THE APARTMENT.

ZOOSH
IT ISN'T MUCH, BUT THIS SHOULD PAY FOR YOUR TROUBLE.

WHAT?!
B-DMP

ESPECIALLY BECAUSE MY DISAPPEARANCE MIGHT LEAD TO MORE UNSAVORY RUMORS ABOUT THE APARTMENT.
PEOPLE MAY EVEN SPECULATE THAT, EVEN IF I DIDN'T DIE IN THE ROOM, YOU'RE TRYING TO HIDE THE FACT THAT I *DID* COMMIT SUICIDE SOMEWHERE.

YEAH ...
BUT ...
CLACK
CLACK
That's a THICK envelope.

PLOP

BUT I SUPPOSE MY COUSIN AND THAT GIRL WILL BE PAYING YOU A VISIT SOON.

IN THAT CASE, SHE WILL GIVE YOU A PERFECTLY LOGICAL EXPLANATION...
...AS TO WHY THERE WAS A SERIES OF SUICIDES IN THE APARTMENT.
YOU WON'T HAVE TO WORRY ABOUT RENTING IT OUT IN THE FUTURE.
WELL THEN, THANK YOU FOR HAVING ME.
TAKE CARE.
TMP
THAK
HEY!

I HOPE THINGS WORK OUT WITH YOUR COUSIN.
TWO DAYS LATER
SKREEE
SKREE
SKREE
EITHER HER INSTINCTS ARE THAT GOOD,
OR SHE MANAGED TO SECURE THIS FUTURE FOR HER-SELF.
WAFT

EITHER WAY, SHE'S ONE STEP AHEAD OF US. SHE GOT AWAY.
SORRY TO BOTHER YOU ON A WEEKEND MORNING.
I AM KOTOKO IWANAGA.
THIS IS RIKKA SAKURAGAWA-SAN'S COUSIN, KURÔ SAKURA-GAWA-SAN.
HE IS ALSO MY BOY-FRIEND.
THANK YOU FOR TAKING CARE OF RIKKA-SAN.
THIS IS THE HORRIBLE GIRL...?
IS THERE SOMETHING ABOUT ME THAT BOTHERS YOU?

OH.
NO, UM.
IT'S NOTHING.
IT'S JUST, FROM WHAT SAKURAGAWA-SAN TOLD ME, I HAD A DIFFERENT IMPRESSION OF YOU.
I DIDN'T EXPECT HER COUSIN'S GIRLFRIEND TO LOOK LIKE SUCH A REFINED LITTLE DOLL.
A DOLL, HE SAYS! I'LL HAVE YOU KNOW THERE'S BLOOD IN THESE VEINS.
BESIDES, IWANAGA IS PRETTY HAIRY.
NOT LIKE A DOLL AT ALL.
WHO ARE YOU CALLING HAIRY?!
THWACK
YOU KNOW THAT IS A BALD-FACED LIE!
DID YOU NOT ONCE DEEPLY LAMENT, AND I QUOTE...
"GUESS I CAN NEVER DRINK SEAWEED WINE WITH YOU!"

SO SHE MOVED INTO A STIGMATIZED PROPERTY. THAT MAY HAVE BEEN A BLIND SPOT.

STILL, RIKKA-SAN IS LIKE A SNAKE WITH A WOMAN'S HEAD. WHY DO SO MANY PEOPLE SEEM TO LIKE HER?

CLANG カン

CLANG カン

YOU JUST HAVE AN EXCESSIVE *DIS*LIKE OF HER.

CLANG カン

AND WHY DO YOU KEEP TAKING YOUR COUSIN'S SIDE OVER YOUR GIRLFRIEND'S?

SO, UM.
WHY EXACTLY ARE YOU LOOKING FOR HER?
SHE DIDN'T SEEM LIKE A BAD PERSON.
AND AREN'T YOU THE ONES MAKING IT SO SHE HAS TO GO INTO HIDING?
IT'S NOT LIKE WE'RE TRYING TO CATCH HER AND EAT HER.
YOU MIGHT SAY THAT LETTING HER ROAM FREE WOULD CAUSE SOME SOCIETAL PROBLEMS.
IT JUST WOULDN'T BE RIGHT.
KA-CHAK
ガチャ
IF ANYTHING, RIKKA-SAN IS THE ONE THAT'S PUT *US* IN A BIND.
DID SHE SAY ANYTHING ABOUT WHAT SHE PLANS TO DO NEXT? EVEN SOMETHING VAGUE?

LET'S SEE...
IT'D PROBABLY BE BETTER NOT TO TELL THEM WHAT SHE SAID ABOUT THEM.
OR THAT SHE'S TRYING TO BREAK THEM UP.
...ALL SHE EVER TOLD US WAS THAT SHE'D COME HERE TO SETTLE DOWN AND THINK OF HER NEXT PLAN, BUT I DON'T KNOW ANY MORE THAN THAT.
パカ
KA-POP
WE MANAGED TO FIND HER THIS TIME BECAUSE SHE STAYED IN ONE PLACE FOR SO LONG.
BUT SHE WON'T MAKE THAT MISTAKE TWICE.
ば
WHOOSH
WHEW
THIS IS SO ANNOYING.
I suppose we can't expect her to leave any clues...
THANK YOU FOR YOUR ASSISTANCE.

Kotoko Iwanaga
xxx-xxxx-xxxx
xxx@xxx.xxx
PLEASE CONTACT ME IF YOU REMEMBER ANYTHING ABOUT RIKKA-SAN.
AND IF YOU HAVE ANY OTHER PROBLEMS, THEN YOU'RE WELCOME TO CALL ME ANYTIME.

SHE WILL GIVE YOU A PERFECTLY LOGICAL EXPLANA-TION.
...

OF COURSE. YOUR PRESENT CONCERN IS THIS STIGMATIZED PROPERTY, YES?

OH!

DON'T TROUBLE YOUR-SELF OVER IT. THERE WERE NEVER ANY CURSES, NO GHOSTS— NOTHING UN-USUAL HAS EVER POSSESSED THIS APARTMENT.
THE DEATHS SHOULD STOP AS LONG AS YOU DON'T RENT IT TO ANYONE WITH SUICIDAL THOUGHTS.

THE LOW RENT CONTRIBUTED TO THE SERIES OF TRAGEDIES, AS WELL.
IT WAS NO MORE THAN A SERIES OF UNFORTUNATE COINCIDENCES.
WHAT? BUT...
TROT
TROT
THE FIRST SUICIDE HAPPENED FOR OBVIOUS REASONS.
THE SECOND VICTIM WAS IN A WEAKENED MENTAL STATE, TOO, SO THERE WAS NOTHING UNUSUAL ABOUT HER DEATH.
THAT'S WHAT SAKURAGAWA-SAN WAS SAYING...
BUT THAT DOESN'T EXPLAIN THE THIRD VICTIM.
WHY WOULD THE SECOND VICTIM'S EX-BOYFRIEND GO OUT OF HIS WAY TO RENT THIS APARTMENT AND KILL HIMSELF THREE MONTHS LATER?
FSH
BECAUSE THE MAN HAD TO BE SURE.

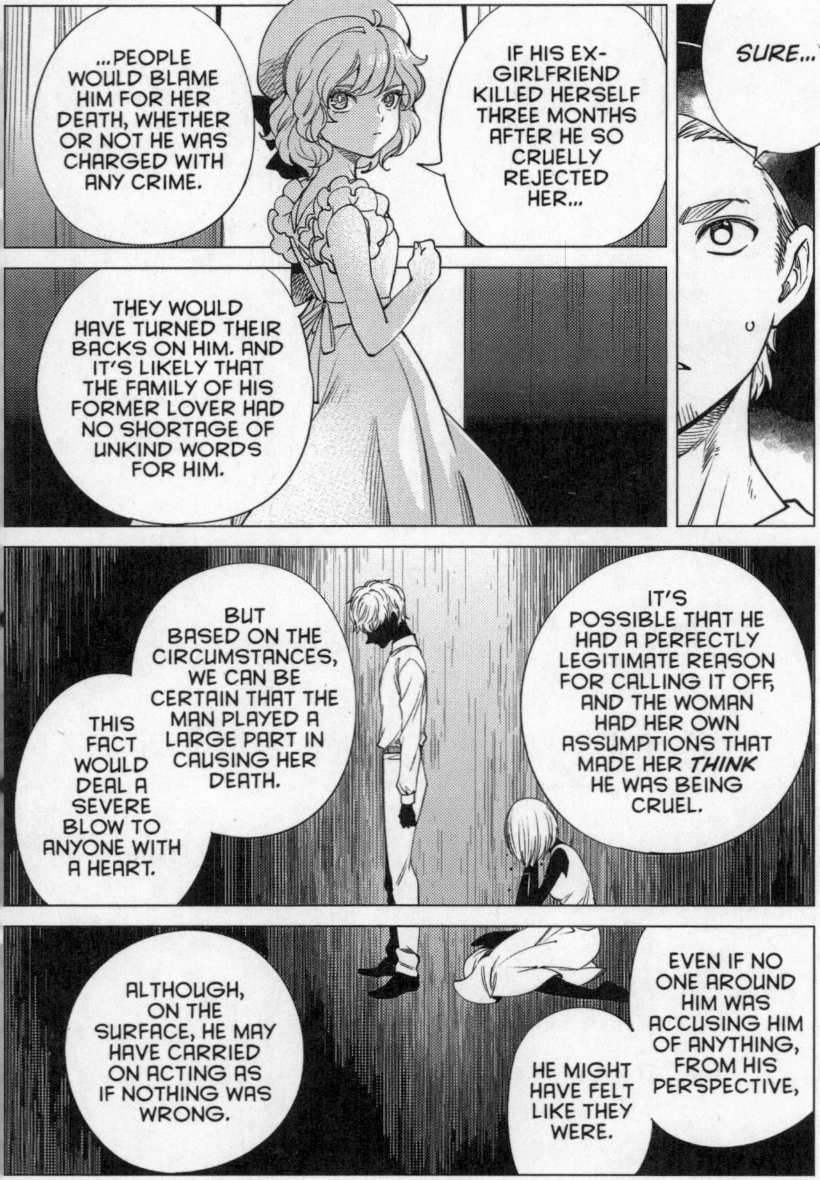

IF HIS EX-GIRLFRIEND KILLED HERSELF THREE MONTHS AFTER HE SO CRUELLY REJECTED HER...
...PEOPLE WOULD BLAME HIM FOR HER DEATH, WHETHER OR NOT HE WAS CHARGED WITH ANY CRIME.
THEY WOULD HAVE TURNED THEIR BACKS ON HIM. AND IT'S LIKELY THAT THE FAMILY OF HIS FORMER LOVER HAD NO SHORTAGE OF UNKIND WORDS FOR HIM.
SURE...?

WELL, THAT'S TRUE.
HE'D HAVE TO BE INCREDIBLY HEARTLESS TO NOT FEEL ANY GUILT.
BUT DOESN'T THAT MEAN HE HAS MORE REASON *NOT* TO RENT THE APART-MENT WHERE SHE KILLED HERSELF?
IT WOULD JUST MAKE THE GUILT THAT MUCH WORSE.
LIKE I SAID, THE MAN HAD TO BE SURE.
HE HAD TO BE SURE THAT IT WASN'T HIS FAULT SHE DIED—THAT THERE WAS SOMETHING IN THE APARTMENT THAT KILLED HER.
IT WAS THAT VERY GUILT THAT BROUGHT HIM HERE, TO FIND SOMETHING HE COULD SHIFT THE BLAME ONTO.

Paranormal Special

Strange Rumors of Stigmatized Properties

SOME SUPERNATURAL POWER WAS AT WORK IN THE ROOM, DRIVING ITS TENANTS TO THEIR DEATHS.

THE SERIES OF SUICIDES IN THAT APARTMENT STARTED YEARS AGO, THE HAIR OF THE DECEASED IS BURIED IN THE WALLS AND CEILING, ETC. ETC.

THOSE KINDS OF RUMORS ARE EASILY EXAG-GERATED AND BLOWN OUT OF PROPORTION.

YEAH.

I DID HEAR STORIES LIKE THAT.

Apartment Shop
Apartments for Rent
☆Lots of natural lighting
☆Low rent, no deposit
Green residential street
Apartments for Rent
THE MAN IN QUESTION GOT WIND OF THOSE RUMORS...
...AND THOUGHT, "IT'S THE APARTMENT'S FAULT MY EX KILLED HERSELF."
"MAYBE I DON'T HAVE TO TAKE THE BLAME FOR THIS AFTER ALL."
HE WANTED TO MAKE SURE THERE REALLY WAS A SPIRIT HERE.
AND THAT'S WHY HE MOVED IN.
EVEN IF THERE WAS ACTUALLY A GHOST, HE COULDN'T BE SURE HIS FRIENDS AND ASSOCIATES WOULD BELIEVE IT.
BUT IF HE EXPERIENCED IT PERSONALLY...
...HE COULD BE CERTAIN THAT, "THE SUICIDE WASN'T MY FAULT."
"IT WAS THAT *THING'S* FAULT."
IT WOULD EASE HIS GUILT CONSIDERABLY.

AND ONCE HE WAS SURE THAT THERE WAS SOMETHING HAUNTING THE APARTMENT, HE WOULD LEAVE.

ONCE HE WAS SURE...?
WOULDN'T IT BE WORSE TO KNOW SUCH THINGS REALLY EXIST?

HE WOULD HAVE ALSO FELT THE ACCUSING STARES OF THE PEOPLE AROUND HIM.
DIFFERENT PEOPLE ARE AFRAID OF DIFFERENT THINGS.

PEOPLE ASSUME THAT WHEN SOME-THING SPIRITUAL IN NATURE IS HAUNTING A PLACE, IT HAS NO POWER OVER THEM ONCE THEY LEAVE.
IN CONTRAST, THE GUILT IN HIS HEART WOULD ALWAYS BE WITH HIM—HE WOULD NEVER ESCAPE IT.

AND TO THIS MAN AT THIS TIME, AT LEAST...
...I SUSPECT HIS GUILT SCARED HIM MORE THAN ANY SPECTRE.
SO WHY DID HE KILL HIMSELF?
IF HE WAS GOING TO LEAVE THE APARTMENT AS SOON AS HE FOUND SOMETHING HAUNTING IT, WHAT COULD HAVE PRESSURED HIM INTO SUICIDE?
YOU HAVE IT BACK-WARDS.

THERE WAS NOTHING HAUNTING THE APARTMENT.
HE WAS DRIVEN TO HIS DEATH BECAUSE THREE MONTHS HAD PASSED WITH NO SIGN OF PARANORMAL ACTIVITY.

THE LACK OF ANYTHING UNUSUAL SOLIDIFIED THE IDEA IN HIS MIND THAT HIS EX-GIRLFRIEND'S DEATH WASN'T CAUSED BY THE APARTMENT.
HE HAD CAUSED IT HIMSELF.

HE PRACTICALLY TRIPPED OVER HIMSELF TO MOVE INTO THIS APARTMENT AND FIND A SCAPE-GOAT.
BUT INSTEAD HE WAS FORCED TO ACCEPT THAT THERE WAS NO SCAPEGOAT TO BE FOUND.

AND SO HIS GUILT GREW ALL THE LARGER, UNTIL HIS HEART COULD NO LONGER ESCAPE IT.

THE GUILT HE HAD SO DESPERATELY TRIED TO AVOID CAME CRASHING DOWN IN FULL FORCE.
THAT MIGHT MAKE ANYONE WISH FOR DEATH.
SO HE DIDN'T KILL HIMSELF BECAUSE OF SOMETHING WEIRD IN THE ROOM...
...BUT BECAUSE THERE *WASN'T* ANYTHING WEIRD?
IT MAY BE THAT HE DIDN'T LEAVE A NOTE BECAUSE HE WAS TOO DISTRAUGHT TO WRITE ONE.
OR MAYBE, HE CHOSE TO DIE WITHOUT A NOTE...
...IN AN EFFORT TO SHOW THE OTHER PEOPLE IN HIS LIFE THAT HE, TOO, HAD BEEN DRIVEN TO SUICIDE BY SOME SUPERNATURAL POWER IN THE APARTMENT.

"THERE IS SOMETHING PARANORMAL IN THIS ROOM, AND THAT'S WHAT KILLED MY EX-GIRLFRIEND."
"IT HAD NOTHING TO DO WITH ME."
THAT'S WHAT HE WANTED PEOPLE TO THINK.

IT WAS HIS LAST STAND—HIS FINAL ATTEMPT TO AT LEAST STOP THE ACCUSATIONS AGAINST HIM AFTER HIS DEATH.

TALK ABOUT STUB-BORN.
BUT HE MAY HAVE ALSO SUCCEEDED IN MITIGATING THE SHAME THAT HE CAUSED HIS FAMILY.

IF THE ONLY EXPLANATION IS THAT HE PRACTICALLY PUSHED A GIRL TO HER DEATH, THEN KILLED HIMSELF,
THEN THOSE LEFT BEHIND WOULD FEEL NOTHING BUT PAIN KNOWING WHAT ONE OF THEIR RELATIVES HAD DONE.

YOU MIGHT SEE THIS AS A FINAL ACT OF KINDNESS TO THEM—HE'S GIVEN THEM A WAY TO ESCAPE THAT PAIN,
EVEN WHEN HE HIMSELF HAD NO ESCAPE, EXCEPT THROUGH DEATH.

ANYWAY, IT'S A GOOD EXAMPLE OF HOW IT DOESN'T PAY TO BELIEVE IN SPIRITS OR YÔKAI.

I DON'T KNOW, I THOUGHT THEY GOT ALONG PRETTY WELL.
BEEP

YEAH. I REALLY GOT THE FEELING THAT SAKURAGAWA-SAN'S COUSIN CARES FOR IWANAGA-SAN.
Like when they stood up.
And when he helped her on the stairs.

BUT THAT IWANAGA-SAN, SHE'S...
Hmmm...

WAAH!
WAAH!
WAAH!
PRETTY HORRIBLE.
YEAH.

THINGS MIGHT LOOK PRETTY GOOD NOW, BUT YOU NEVER KNOW WHAT COULD HAPPEN.

LANTERN: ODEN

BESIDES, YOU KNOW NO SPIRIT WOULD HAUNT AN APARTMENT WITH RIKKA-SAN LIVING IN IT.
...
SHE'S JUST LIKE YOU, SENPAI. FROM THE SPECTRES' POINT OF VIEW, SHE'S A DREADFUL, FOUL-SMELLING MONSTER.
ドド
BOOM
ANY CREATURE THAT MAY HAVE BEEN HAUNTING THE PLACE WOULD HAVE LEFT.
BUT THEN I WOULD HAVE GOTTEN A REPORT ABOUT HER MUCH SOONER.

ドーン
BOOM
PATTER
パラパラ
PATTER

WE NEED TO HURRY AND STOP HER.

ドン
BOOM
SPARKLE
キラキラ
SPARKLE
BUT I DO WONDER HOW RIKKA-SAN DESCRIBED ME TO THEM.
I'M ABSOLUTELY CERTAIN THAT SHE PAINTED ME AS A HORRIBLE PERSON.
I THINK YOU BEING SOMEONE WHO KNOWS NO FEAR IS PRETTY HORRIBLE.

OH, PLEASE. I HAVE FEARS.
LIKE?
RUNG
I DON'T LIKE THOSE BIG FIRE BELLS.
EVERY-THING ALWAYS GOES *RUNG* WITH THEM.

SISSS
...
IS THAT FROM THE RAKUGO *KAEN DAIKO*?
BOOM
THAT'S MY KURÔ-SENPAI. SO DIFFERENT FROM RIKKA-SAN.
PATTER
PATTER

AND QUIT BLOWING SMOKE BY GIVING AWAY RAKUGO PUNCHLINES.
YOUR WORDPLAY ISN'T ANYWHERE NEAR AS ADVANCED AS YOU THINK.
Yeah, but...
I still can't think of anything...
TUG

THINGS WORK OUT BETTER BETWEEN MEN AND WOMEN WHEN THEY HAVE A SECRET OR TWO.

RATTLE

RATTLE

ずるる—
SLURRRP
BOWL: UDON NOODLES

SORRY FOR ASKING TO YOU TO MEET ME ON SUCH SHORT NOTICE.
IT'S ALL RIGHT.
IT'S PROBABLY WORSE FOR YOU— I KNOW YOU'RE BUSY RUNNING YOUR BUSI-NESS.
CLATTER
IT'S BEEN WHAT, TWO YEARS, SINCE I LAST SAW YOU?
I THINK I WAS STILL A FRESHMAN AT THE TIME.
MANABU AMACHI COLLEGE THIRD-YEAR
HAS IT BEEN THAT LONG?
I GUESS THAT HAPPENS WHEN YOU'RE JUST AN UNCLE.
KÔYA FUJINUMA
SO WHAT'S SO IMPORTANT THAT MY MOM'S ESTEEMED BROTHER HAS INVITED ME OUT TO LUNCH?

YOU WENT TO EIEI PRIVATE HIGH SCHOOL, RIGHT?
DO YOU KNOW ANYTHING ABOUT KOTOKO IWANAGA?
KOTOKO IWA-NAGA?
SURELY YOU'VE AT LEAST HEARD OF HER. SHE'S THE HEIRESS OF THE IWANAGA FAMILY. I'M LOOKING FOR INFORMATION ON HER.
DID YOU HEAR ANY RUMORS ABOUT HER BACK IN SCHOOL? ANYTHING AT ALL?
EVEN HER FAVORITE FOODS, OR WHAT SHE LOOKS FOR IN A MAN?
I'LL EVEN SETTLE FOR THE NAMES OF HER CLASS-MATES.
OH, IWA-NAGA-SAN.
WHAT HAVE YOU DONE THIS TIME?

CHAPTER 24: "FOR TOMORROW"

IF YOU'RE LOOKING FOR INTEL, CAN'T YOU ASK A DETECTIVE AGENCY?
I'M SURE *YOU* KNOW OF ONE OR TWO YOU CAN TRUST.
DIDN'T YOU KNOW?
THERE ARE A NUMBER OF STRANGE STORIES ABOUT HER.
WHEN DEALING WITH A BUSINESS OR OPERATION INVOLVING THE IWANAGA FAMILY, ANY MISSTEP COULD LEAD TO DISASTER.
ASK THEM FOR ADVICE, ON THE OTHER HAND, AND EVERY-THING COMES TOGETHER.
ESPECIALLY WHEN THE PROBLEM CAN'T BE EXPLAINED— MORE SO IF IT'S SOME SPOOKY, ALMOST SUPER-NATURAL TROUBLE.
IT'S SCARY HOW NEATLY THOSE MATTERS GET RE-SOLVED.
AND WHEN-EVER THAT HAP-PENS...
...YOU'LL FIND THE IWANAGA HEIRESS IN THE SHADOWS, PULLING ALL STRINGS.

PEOPLE HAVE TRIED MANY TIMES IN THE PAST TO INVESTIGATE HER, BUT APPARENTLY SHE'S DISCOVERED EVERY ATTEMPT.

AND NOT JUST TAILS—EVEN WHEN THEY TRIED TO ASK AROUND AT HER USUAL HAUNTS.

SHE WOULD ALWAYS KNOW THE NEXT DAY EXACTLY WHICH COMPANY HIRED WHOM TO DO THE DIGGING.

THAT'S EXACTLY WHY I DON'T WANT TO GET INVOLVED.

I SEE.

NOW NO DETECTIVE AGENCY WORTH ITS SALT WILL TAKE THE JOB.

AND I WOULD PREFER TO AVOID GIVING HER A BAD IMPRESSION OF ME BEFORE THINGS EVEN GET STARTED.

BUT I STILL WANT INFORMATION.

...BEFORE THINGS GET STARTED?

SO MY ONLY OPTION IS TO FIND PEOPLE WHO KNEW HER AND LEARN WHAT I CAN FROM HEARSAY.
SIGH...
I KNOW A FEW THINGS ABOUT IWANAGA-SAN.
SHE WAS IN THE MYSTERY APPRECIATION CLUB WHEN I WAS PRESIDENT.
WHAT?!
REALLY?!
WHICH IS WHY I'M GOING TO HAVE TO WARN YOU THAT MY BEST ADVICE IS TO STAY AWAY FROM HER.
ESPECIALLY IF YOU WANT TO TRICK HER OR TAKE ADVANTAGE OF HER. YOU'LL ONLY GET HURT.
I GOT BURNED FOR THAT MYSELF.
YOU?

BUT IT'S NOT LIKE THERE WAS ANY REAL HARM DONE.
IN FACT, MORE OFTEN THAN NOT, SHE WOUND UP HELPING ME OUT.
BUT I STILL CAN'T SHAKE MY IMPRESSION OF HER.

AT THE TIME, THE MYSTERY CLUB WAS IN DANGER OF BEING DISBANDED.
I WANTED TO KEEP THE CLUB ALIVE, SO I TRIED TO FORCE IWANAGA-SAN TO JOIN...

...SO SHE SAW RIGHT THROUGH ME AND FOILED MY PLOT.
BUT SHE DID END UP JOINING YOUR CLUB, DIDN'T SHE?
THAT MEANS YOU WON, RIGHT?
YES.

AND THANKS TO HER, WE EVEN GOT TWO NEW FIRST-YEARS TO JOIN.

THE CLUB'S CRISIS WAS AVERTED.

WOW! *TWO* NEW MEMBERS!

WE DID IT!

IT'S ALREADY JULY—I'D GIVEN UP ALL HOPE OF NEW MEMBERS!

I LIKE MYSTERIES, BUT I DIDN'T KNOW THERE WAS A CLUB.

FIRST-YEAR REN AKIBA

ME, TOO.

I ONLY FOUND OUT ABOUT IT WHEN I HEARD RUMORS THAT IWANAGA-SAN JOINED.

FIRST-YEAR RENA KAZAMA

SHE CAME TO THE CLUB ROOM THREE TIMES A WEEK.
ON RAINY DAYS, SHE'D USUALLY SLEEP BY THE WINDOW.
AND I GUESS SHE KNEW A LOT ABOUT MYSTERIES BEFORE SHE JOINED, SO I COULDN'T COMPLAIN ABOUT HER QUALIFICATIONS AS A MEMBER.
SHE JUST DOESN'T FIT IN.
SHE'S MORE LIKE THE SYMBOL OF THE MYSTERY CLUB.
OR ITS MAS-COT?
NO, SHE'S NOT THAT CUTE.
ONE DAY IN SECOND TERM, JUST AS THE NEW MEMBERS WERE STARTING TO GET THE HANG OF THINGS...
UM.
A CLASSMATE OF MINE CAME TO ME WITH A PROBLEM THAT HE WANTS THE MYSTERY CLUB TO SOLVE...

OH?

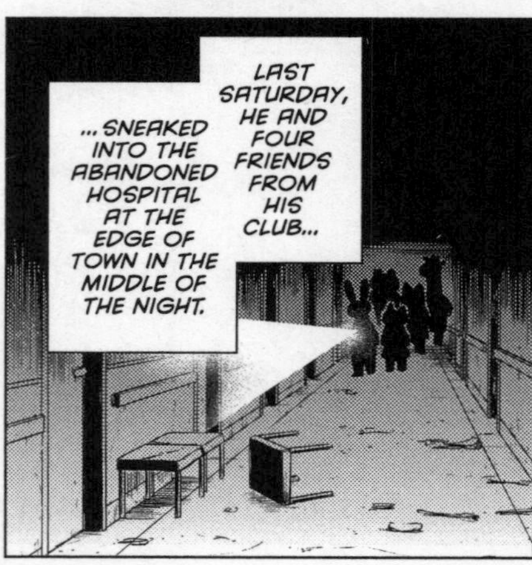
LAST SATURDAY, HE AND FOUR FRIENDS FROM HIS CLUB...
...SNEAKED INTO THE ABANDONED HOSPITAL AT THE EDGE OF TOWN IN THE MIDDLE OF THE NIGHT.

ISN'T THAT THE SUPPOSEDLY HAUNTED ONE?
I'm surprised they had the guts.

YES.
THEY DIDN'T THINK TOO MUCH OF IT—IT WAS BASICALLY JUST A DARE.
IT MAKES ME DOUBT THEIR SANITY.
IT MAY BE ABANDONED, BUT THAT'S STILL TRESPASSING.
SO DID SOMETHING HAPPEN? DID THEY SEE A GHOST?
POING
POING
HE TOLD ME THEY DIDN'T SEE ANYTHING AT THE HOSPITAL.
THEY JUST WENT HOME, LIKE FROM ANY OTHER PLACE.
AAHHH, THAT WAS SO SCARY!

IT'S BEEN THREE DAYS, AND SHE'S STILL STAYING HOME FROM SCHOOL.

AND SHE DOESN'T KNOW WHY SHE FEELS SO BAD,

SO ALL HER FRIENDS ARE SAYING SOMETHING MUST HAVE GOTTEN HER AT THE HOSPITAL.

AND HE WAS WONDERING...

...IF WE COULD DO SOMETHING TO HELP.

ずん
ZHOOM
WE ARE THE MYSTERY CLUB.
PROBLEMS LIKE THAT ARE FOR WEIRDO CLUBS LIKE THE OCCULT CLUB.
ちら
GLANCE
I AGREE WITH YOU, BUT...
パラ
FLIP
YOU KNOW.
BOOK: THE ZOMBIE DETECTIVE 2
MRRGH...
YOU DON'T NEED ANY SPIRITS OR SPECTRES TO EXPLAIN THIS KID'S PROBLEM.
THEY WERE WALKING AROUND AN ABANDONED HOSPITAL AT NIGHT—PROBABLY WEARING LIGHT LAYERS IN THIS HEAT. THEY WERE OBVIOUSLY GONNA GET BITTEN BY BUGS.

THEY'D BE BREATHING IN ALL THE FILTHY DUST AND JUNK IN THE AIR—NOT TO MENTION THE GERMS. THERE'S NO SHORTAGE OF THINGS THAT COULD MAKE A PERSON SICK.
IT'S NO SURPRISE THAT ONE OF THEM ENDED UP STUCK IN BED.
AND IF SHE'S CONVINCED SHE'S POSSESSED, THAT WILL HURT HER PSYCHOLOGICALLY. OF COURSE SHE'LL TAKE LONGER TO RECOVER.

ANOTHER BORING INTERPRETA-TION FROM MANABU-KUN.
YOU MEAN ...
MOST LOGICAL.
GOT IT?

THAT'S HOW WE DO THINGS IN THE MYSTERY CLUB.

BUT EVEN REAL MYSTERY STORIES HAVE PEOPLE THAT TURN OUT TO BE GHOSTS.
OR IT TURNS OUT THE KILLER WAS A WITCH OR SOMETHING.

BOOK: LOCKED ROOM MOUNTAIN; THEY'LL NEVER MAKE IT OUT
THAT IS ONLY ACCEPTABLE BECAUSE IT HAPPENED—*RARELY*—WHEN MOST MYSTERY STORIES WERE STILL FOLLOWING ALL THE RULES.
ONCE YOU START EXPECTING THAT SORT OF THING, IT BECOMES IMPOSSIBLE TO DEFINE THE GENRE.
BOOK: THE ZOMBIE DETECTIVE; MBIEZOZO
ZOOM
THEY ARE THE EXCEPTION, *NEVER* TO BE TAKEN AS THE RULE.
YOU'RE ABSOLUTELY RIGHT, MR. PRESIDENT, AND I GAVE MY CLASSMATE A SIMILAR ANSWER.
BUT HE DID ASK THE ENTIRE CLUB, SO IT WOULDN'T BE FAIR OF ME NOT TO AT LEAST BRING IT UP.
I DON'T LIKE THIS.
HE DID SEEM PRETTY SPOOKED, AFTER ALL.
Hee
Hee
Hee
SHUT

GHOSTS, SPECTRES... WHY DO PEOPLE BELIEVE IN THOSE THINGS, ANYWAY?

SO WHAT YOU'RE SAYING IS, WE NEED A LOGICAL EXPLANATION THAT WILL CONVINCE THIS CLASSMATE OF YOURS AND ASSUAGE HIS FEARS.

PROVIDING SUCH A SOLUTION WOULD BE QUITE IN CHARACTER FOR THE MYSTERY CLUB, NO?

HOW DO YOU LIKE THIS FOR A THEORY?

ABSENT
ABSENT
SHE DIDN'T *"STAY HOME FROM SCHOOL BECAUSE SHE WENT TO A HAUNTED BUILDING."*
BUT RATHER, *"SHE WENT TO A HAUNTED BUILDING SO SHE COULD STAY HOME FROM SCHOOL."*

THE REVERSE APPROACH, EH?

SOMETHING HAPPENED TO THIS FRIEND THAT MADE HER WANT TO PROLONG HER WEEKEND AND STAY HOME FROM SCHOOL.
BUT SHE DIDN'T WANT ANYONE TO KNOW ABOUT IT.

FOR EXAMPLE, HER BOYFRIEND DUMPED HER, AND SHE WANTED TO HIDE IN HER ROOM FOR A WHILE TO DEAL WITH THE SHOCK.
BUT THAT'S AN EMBARRASSING REASON TO STAY HOME FROM SCHOOL, AND SHE WOULDN'T WANT ANYONE'S PITY.
MAYBE SHE'S IN THE MIDDLE OF A VIDEO GAME, AND IT'S GETTING REALLY GOOD, SO SHE WANTS TO KEEP PLAYING, EVEN IF IT MEANS MISSING SCHOOL.
BUT ONCE AGAIN, IT WOULD BE EMBAR-RASSING FOR PEOPLE TO KNOW SHE'S OBSESSED WITH A GAME.
I CAN COME UP WITH ANY NUMBER OF REASONS.
SHE *IS* AT AN AGE WHERE SHE'D WORRY WHAT PEOPLE THINK OF HER.
ESPECIALLY WHEN IT COMES TO NEW FRIENDS THAT SHE JUST MADE IN HIGH SCHOOL, SHE WOULD BE HESITANT TO REVEAL TOO MANY DETAILS ABOUT HER PRIVATE LIFE.
SHE MAY NOT TRUST THEM TO KEEP HER SECRETS SECRET.

SO SHE NEEDED A PLAUSIBLE LIE TO EXPLAIN HER ABSENCE FROM SCHOOL.

BUT THEN COULDN'T SHE JUST TELL PEOPLE THAT SHE HAD A COLD AND NEEDED TO STAY HOME?

THEN SHE HEARD PEOPLE TALKING ABOUT GOING TO THE SUPPOSEDLY HAUNTED HOSPITAL, AND SHE REALIZED SHE SHOULD USE THAT.

IF SHE DID THAT, SHE WOULD HAVE TO ACT LIKE SHE HAD REALLY CAUGHT A COLD.
AND IF PEOPLE CAME TO SEE HOW SHE WAS DOING, THAT WOULD BE EVEN MORE TROUBLE TO DEAL WITH.
ピンポーン
DING DONG

BUT IF SHE WERE POSSESSED, THE SPOOKY CIRCUMSTANCES WOULD MAKE PEOPLE THINK TWICE ABOUT VISITING, AND THEY WOULDN'T BE INTERESTED IN CALLING, EITHER.

PEOPLE ONLY THINK HAUNTED BUILDINGS ARE FUN IF NOBODY GETS HURT.

BUT IF SOMETHING ***DOES*** HAPPEN TO SOMEONE THEY KNOW, THEN THEY'LL AVOID EVEN TALKING ABOUT IT, AT LEAST FOR A LITTLE WHILE.

SO NO ONE WOULD EVER FIND OUT THE REAL REASON YOUR CLASSMATE'S FRIEND SKIPPED SCHOOL.

EXPLAIN THAT TO YOUR CLASSMATE, AND I'M SURE HE'LL FEEL BETTER.

す SFF

コッ CLACK

AND ALSO,

IT MAY BE A GOOD IDEA TO TELL HIM NOT TO ASK TOO MANY QUESTIONS IF HIS FRIEND ***DOES*** COME BACK TO SCHOOL IN PERFECT HEALTH.

コッ CLACK

IF HIS FRIEND WANTS TO HIDE SOMETHING, IT WOULD BE CRUEL TO PRY.

IN SOME SITUATIONS, THESE MATTERS TURN OUT TO BE GRAVER THAN YOU EVER IMAGINED. HE MAY END UP SEEING INTO THE DARKNESS OF HIS FRIEND'S HEART.

UH...

RIGHT.

GOT IT.

BOOK: THE ZOMBIE DETECTIVE; TO HOKKAIDO

WELL, SHE'S CLEARLY A THINKING WOMAN.

Hmm...

AND IT SOUNDS LIKE SHE DOESN'T BELIEVE IN GHOSTS?

I DON'T KNOW ABOUT THAT.

OUR CLUB MEMBER WENT BACK TO HER CLASSMATE THE NEXT DAY AND TOLD HIM IWANAGA-SAN'S THEORY.

THE DAY AFTER THAT...

HIS SICK FRIEND REALLY DID COME BACK TO SCHOOL IN FULL HEALTH.

SHE CLAIMED SHE FELT MUCH BETTER ALL OF A SUDDEN.

AS PER IWANAGA-SAN'S INSTRUCTIONS, THE CLASSMATE REFRAINED FROM ASKING HIS FRIEND WHY SHE HAD STAYED HOME.

HE JUST LAUGHED ABOUT HOW THERE WAS NO SUCH THING AS GHOSTS.

?

...IT SOUNDS LIKE THINGS ALMOST WENT *TOO* WELL.

BUT EVEN IF THE FRIEND REALLY WAS JUST UNDER THE WEATHER, SHE COULD HAVE RECOVERED QUICKLY. IT MIGHT STILL BE A COIN-CIDENCE.

IWANAGA-SAN SAID THE SAME THING.

I NEVER DID FIND OUT HOW MUCH OF HER THEORY WAS CORRECT.

IT DIDN'T HELP THAT SHE MADE SURE TO TELL PEOPLE NOT TO PRESS THE GIRL FOR ANSWERS.

IN-DEED.

SHE COVERED ALL HER BASES.

MUNCH MUNCH

...

DONE SOMETHING? LIKE WHAT?
...YOU KNOW, I THINK IWANAGA-SAN *MUST* HAVE SECRETLY DONE SOMETHING ABOUT THAT SICK FRIEND.
Mystery Appreciation Club
MAYBE THE FRIEND REALLY *WAS* POSSESSED BY SOME WEIRD GHOST...
...AND SHE GOT BETTER BECAUSE IWANAGA-SAN CONVINCED THE GHOST TO GO AWAY.

ZWOOSH
DON'T BASE YOUR THEORIES ON THE IDEA THAT GHOSTS REALLY EXIST.
"CON-VINCED" IT?
IN THAT CASE, A MORE LIKELY THEORY IS THAT SHE HAD A REALLY GOOD DOCTOR SENT TO THE FRIEND'S HOUSE TO TREAT HER.
AND THEN BRIBED OR BLACK-MAILED HER INTO KEEPING QUIET ABOUT IT.
THAT IS *NOT* MORE LIKELY. IWANAGA-SAN WAS UNDER NO OBLIGATION TO HIRE A DOCTOR FOR SOME-ONE.
ぱ
SNATCH
WELL, SHE WAS UNDER NO OBLIGATION TO TALK TO A GHOST, EITHER.
...
BUT THINKING ON THOSE LINES, SHE ALSO WAS UNDER NO OBLIGATION TO PROVIDE A THEORY THAT WAS SO CONVENIENT FOR THE CLUB, EITHER.

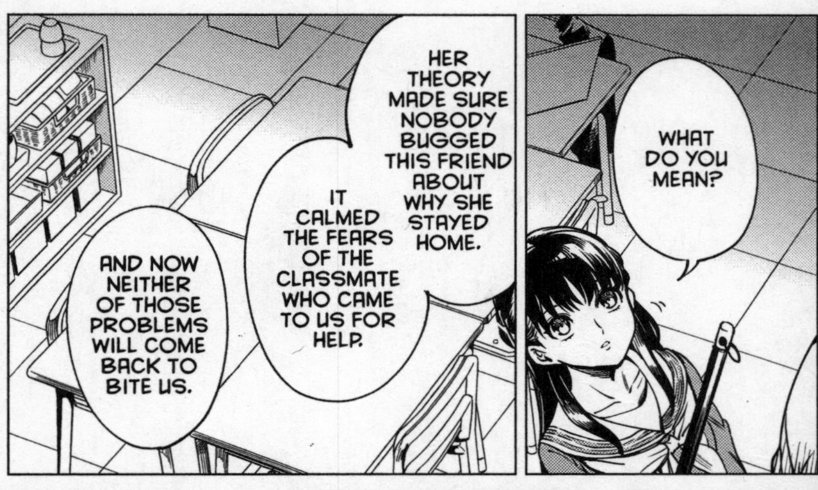
WHAT DO YOU MEAN?
HER THEORY MADE SURE NOBODY BUGGED THIS FRIEND ABOUT WHY SHE STAYED HOME.
IT CALMED THE FEARS OF THE CLASSMATE WHO CAME TO US FOR HELP.
AND NOW NEITHER OF THOSE PROBLEMS WILL COME BACK TO BITE US.

YEAH.
THAT'S TRUE.
THE MYSTERY CLUB GAVE THEM A LOGICAL AND INTER-ESTING ANSWER.
AND HER ANSWER DIDN'T TAKE THE GHOST THING SERIOUSLY, SO NO ONE'S GOING TO START THINKING WE'RE A WEIRDO CLUB.

IF SHE HADN'T DONE THAT, WE MIGHT HAVE STARTED ATTRACTING OCCULT FREAKS WHO HAVE NO INTEREST IN MYSTERY LITERATURE AT ALL.
AND IF THAT HAD HAPPENED, THE MEMBERS WE DO HAVE MIGHT HAVE ABANDONED US, AND THE MYSTERY CLUB WOULD HAVE LOST ITS TRUE PURPOSE.

IT DOESN'T MATTER HOW ACCURATE HER THEORY WAS. SHE TOOK ALL OF OUR CIRCUMSTANCES INTO ACCOUNT AND GAVE THE MOST APPROPRIATE ANSWER.

I SEE. SO IWANAGA-SAN WAS THINKING OF OUR CLUB, TOO, WHEN SHE CAME UP WITH HER SOLUTION.
She's so nice.
IF MY THEORY IS RIGHT, THAT MEANS IWANAGA-SAN WAS ABLE TO FIGURE ALL OF THAT OUT ON THE SPOT.
SHE'S INSCRUTABLE.

BUT IT ONLY WORKED BECAUSE THE FRIEND CAME BACK TWO DAYS LATER IN PERFECT HEALTH, JUST LIKE IWANAGA-SAN PREDICTED.
IF SHE WERE STILL STAYING HOME FROM SCHOOL, KIDS WOULD GET EVEN MORE SCARED.
PEOPLE MIGHT HAVE EVEN STARTED CALLING OUR CLUB INTO QUESTION.

IT'S FINE IF SHE DIDN'T CARE ABOUT THE CLUB, AND JUST SAID WHATEVER POPPED INTO HER HEAD.
BUT IF SHE DID CARE, THEN HOW COULD SHE BE SO SURE IT WOULD WORK?

DID SHE JUST ASSUME THE ODDS WERE IN HER FAVOR...?
カチ TICK
TOCK コチ
MAYBE SHE REALLY *DID* DO SOMETHING?
SO WE'RE BACK TO THAT, EH?

ANYWAY, WHILE IT WAS THE BEST THEORY, IT WAS ALSO A RISK.
BUT EVERYTHING WENT EXACTLY THE WAY SHE SAID IT WOULD.
THAT IS THE REAL MYSTERY.
ぐぐぐぐ
GR-GR-GR-GRRG
Wariness
WHAT IS SHE PLOTTING BY BEING IN OUR CLUB, AND WHY IS SHE BEING SO GOOD TO US?
NO ONE WOULD HAVE CARED IF SHE'D JUST IGNORED THE WHOLE HAUNTED HOSPITAL THING.
GASP

WHAT IF SHE FELL IN LOVE WITH YOU AT FIRST SIGHT, AND NOW SHE'S TRYING TO HELP THE MAN SHE ADORES?!

I GET THE FEELING SHE'S COLD TO PEOPLE IN GENERAL.
I WOULDN'T SAY I'M COLD IN GENERAL, BUT I'M CERTAINLY NOT INTERESTED IN YOU, PRESIDENT.
CLACK
AAAAHH!
I— IWANAGA-SAN!
I DON'T KNOW HOW MUCH OF THAT YOU OVERHEARD, BUT WE COULD REALLY USE SOME ANSWERS HERE.
I STARTED LISTENING FROM ABOUT WHERE YOU TWO STARTED TAKING ADVANTAGE OF YOUR ALONE TIME TO ENGAGE IN INDECENT ACTIVITIES.
HIDE
WHAT ABOUT THIS LOOKS INDECENT TO YOU?

I—
I WON'T LET YOU HAVE MANABU-KUN!
...
I TOLD YOU, I AM NOT INTER-ESTED.
CLATTER
SCRNSH くしゃ
WHERE TO BEGIN?
SIGH...
THERE'S A MAN FOR WHOM I HAVE HARBORED AN UNREQUITED LOVE SINCE MIDDLE SCHOOL.
WHAT ARE YOU TALKING ABOUT? SERIOUSLY.
I AM *TALKING* ABOUT HOW I AM IN LOVE WITH SOMEONE ELSE.
You do NOT have such endearing emotions.
HE IS CURRENTLY A COLLEGE STUDENT, AND HE HAS A GIRLFRIEND.

...A TALL, MATURE, OLDER WOMAN.
WOW, YOU HAVE NO CHANCE.
WHICH IS WHY, IF I WERE TO CONFESS MY FEELINGS TO HIM NOW, HE WOULD ONLY TURN ME DOWN. FURTHERMORE, I'D LEAVE A BAD IMPRESSION AND IT WOULD ALL BE OVER.
You have no chance.
You have no chance.
You have no chance.
BAM
SO FOR NOW MY ONLY OPTION IS TO WAIT FOR HIM TO BREAK UP WITH HER!
MY ONLY OP-TION!
GRG
GRG
SO WHAT IF THERE ARE RUMORS ABOUT THEM PLANNING AN ENGAGEMENT CEREMONY ?!
GRG
GRG
GRG
GRIND
GRIND
GRIND
I MUST BELIEVE THAT MY OPPORTU-NITY WILL ARISE!
You have less than no chance...

SO DOES THIS HAVE ANYTHING TO DO WITH WHY YOU JOINED OUR CLUB?

I AM *TELLING* YOU.

IF, WHILE I AM WAITING FOR MY VERY UNLIKELY CHANCE, I WERE TO ACTIVELY STAND IN THE WAY OF TWO PEOPLE IN LOVE...

...KARMA WILL PREVENT *MY* LOVE FROM EVER COMING TO FRUITION!

MY OP-PORTUNITY WILL NEVER COME!

?

TWANG

YOU'RE RIGHT!

THE GODS OF LOVE NEVER HELP THOSE KINDS OF PEOPLE.

CLENCH

YOU KNOW THEY'VE SAID SINCE ANCIENT TIMES THAT TERRIBLE THINGS ARE IN STORE FOR THOSE WHO TRY TO THWART OTHERS' LOVE.
I DO SEEM TO REMEMBER HER SAYING SOMETHING LIKE THAT...
I DIDN'T THINK SHE WAS ACTUALLY SERIOUS.
THAT IS WHY I AM DOING GOOD DEEDS TO HELP PEOPLE IN LOVE. I PRAY THAT I WILL RECEIVE LIBERAL COMPENSATION.

IN OTHER WORDS, YOU'RE ONLY IN THE CLUB FOR YOUR OWN BENEFIT.
BUT KNOWING YOU, I DON'T THINK YOU NEED TO WAIT FOR THE GODS—I BET YOU COULD PULL SOME STRINGS AND BREAK THEM UP YOURSELF.
AND YOU WOULDN'T HAVE ANY SCRUPLES ABOUT IT, EITHER.
WHAT KIND OF A PERSON DO YOU TAKE ME FOR?
I MEAN, OF COURSE I THOUGHT OF THAT, BUT IF HE WERE TO FIND OUT ABOUT IT LATER, THE DAMAGE WOULD BE IRREPA-RABLE.
THIS IS ONE SITUATION WHERE I CANNOT TAKE EVEN THE SMALLEST RISK.
I wasn't going to tell you ALL of this, but I don't want Kobayashi-san worrying.
SO NOW MY ONLY CHOICE IS TO SIT TIGHT.
THAT'S the kind of person I take you for.
IF SHE'S BEING THAT CAREFUL...
...SHE MUST BE VERY ATTACHED TO THIS GUY.

OKAY, SO TELL US ABOUT THE HAUNTED HOSPITAL INCIDENT.
ばん
BAM
IF YOU'RE TRYING TO BUILD UP GOOD KARMA, YOU WOULDN'T JUST THROW OUT RANDOM THEORIES THAT COULD PUT THE CLUB AT RISK.
WAS IT REALLY A COINCIDENCE THAT THIS FRIEND HOPPED RIGHT BACK TO SCHOOL TWO DAYS LATER?
WHO CAN SAY?
I *MAY* HAVE PULLED SOME STRINGS THERE.

SO SHE HELPED YOU BECAUSE OF HER OWN UNREQUITED LOVE.
THAT'S ADORABLE.
HA HA HA.
SHE OBSESSED FOR YEARS OVER A GUY WHO WAS ALREADY ENGAGED...
SECRETLY SPIED ON HIM AND WISHED FOR HIM TO BREAK UP WITH HIS FIANCÉE. HOW IS THAT ADORABLE?
Well...
WHEN YOU PUT IT THAT WAY...
...
THEN, IN HER SECOND YEAR, WE FOUND OUT THAT THIS CRUSH OF HERS—NOT LONG BEFORE HIS WEDDING—REALLY DID BREAK UP WITH HIS GIRLFRIEND.
SHE WASTED NO TIME GETTING CLOSE TO HIM.
WOW...
AND BY THE TIME SHE WAS A THIRD-YEAR, I HEARD THE TWO OF THEM WERE OFFICIALLY DATING.

OH HO HO HO HO!
YOU CAN IMAGINE HOW THRILLED SHE WAS BACK THEN.
LA LA LA!
LA LA LA!
TWIRLY-WHIRLY-WHIRL
SHE TALKED ABOUT HER NEW BOYFRIEND ALL THE TIME.
OH HO HO HO!
OH HO HO HO HOOO HO HO!
I'm scared
IS THIS REALLY OKAY?!
SHUDDER
I THOUGHT YOU WERE ALL FOR IT!
Hello...
Whoa!
HOOOO HO HO HO HO!
SHUDDER
I WAS, BUT THIS IS JUST SCARY!

THAT *IS* A LITTLE FRIGHTEN-ING.

PEOPLE KEPT COMING TO THE MYSTERY CLUB WITH THEIR ANNOYING PROBLEMS AFTER THAT.

AND THEY WERE PRETTY MUCH ALL SOLVED TO HER SPECIFICA-TIONS.

THERE WERE SOME CASES WHERE I HAD NO IDEA HOW HER SOLUTION COULD HAVE WORKED.

YOU MAY THINK YOU HAVE A PLAN, BUT IF YOU GET CLOSE TO HER, SHE'LL SEE RIGHT THROUGH YOU AND DEAL WITH YOU ACCORD-INGLY.

SO YOU'RE TELLING ME NOT TO RISK PROVOKING THE YOUNG LADY.

BUT WAIT, IF SHE'S SO ATTACHED TO THAT BOYFRIEND OF HERS,
COULD I GET HIM ON MY SIDE,
AND CONTROL THE HEIRESS THROUGH HIM?
I DON'T KNOW IF SHE'S STILL DATING HIM.
EVEN IF SHE IS, I THINK YOU'D RISK INCURRING HER WRATH.
GOOD POINT.
ぎし
CREAK
SHE DOESN'T SOUND LIKE THE TYPE TO BE AMUSED BY SOMETHING LIKE THAT.
HRRRM...
DOES THAT MEAN IT WOULD BE DANGEROUS TO TRY TO GET IN HER GOOD GRACES?
SO...
WHY EXACTLY DO YOU NEED INFORMATION ON IWANAGA-SAN?

I CAN'T GIVE YOU ANY DETAILS, BUT IT'S A MATTER OF INHERITANCE.
INHERI-TANCE?

MURMUR
...WAIT.
WHO DIED?
DON'T TELL ME GRAND-PA DOESN'T HAVE MUCH TIME!
OH, NO. IT'S NO ONE RELATED TO YOU.

IT'S MY WIFE'S FATHER— MY FATHER-IN-LAW. I ASSUME YOU'VE HEARD THE NAME *GÔICHI OTONASHI*?

HE'S THE CHAIRMAN AND CEO OF THAT FAMOUS HOTEL CHAIN, RIGHT?

YEAH.

YES, AND IT'S NOT JUST A DOMESTIC CHAIN—THEY OPERATE ON A GLOBAL SCALE.

HE IS NOW 81 YEARS OLD, AND HE'S HAVING SOME PROBLEMS WITH HIS HEALTH. HE'S STEPPED DOWN FROM MOST OF HIS ADMINI-STRATIVE DUTIES,

BUT HIS FORTUNE IS JUST AS LARGE AS YOU WOULD EXPECT.

SO HE'S STARTED TALKING ABOUT WHAT'S GOING TO HAPPEN TO THAT FORTUNE WHEN HE DIES.

AND LATELY, HE'S GIVEN A RATHER ODD ASSIGNMENT TO DETERMINE HOW HE WILL DIVIDE IT UP.

I COULDN'T AGREE WITH YOU MORE. BUT WE'RE ALREADY PAST THE STAGE OF WORRYING ABOUT A POTENTIAL MURDER.
I CAN'T GIVE YOU ANY DETAILS ABOUT THE ASSIGN-MENT.
ALL I CAN TELL YOU IS THAT WHO-EVER DOES THE BEST JOB WILL BE GIVEN PRIORITY WHEN HE SPLITS THE INHERITANCE.
CHAIRMAN OTONASHI HAS THREE CHILDREN, INCLUDING MY WIFE.
HIS WIFE PASSED AWAY YEARS AGO,
SO THOSE THREE WILL BE THE LEGAL HEIRS.
CHAIRMAN OTONASHI
MRS. OTONASHI
FIRSTBORN SON
FIRSTBORN DAUGHTER
SECOND SON
OF COURSE HE WON'T DO ANYTHING SO RASH AS TO LEAVE THE ENTIRE FORTUNE TO ONLY ONE OF THEM.
AND IT'S NOT ONLY MONEY— HIS ASSETS INCLUDE REAL ESTATE, STOCKS, WORKS OF ART, ANTIQUES, AND SO ON AND SO FORTH.

SOME OF THESE THINGS WILL GO UP IN VALUE AS TIME GOES ON, WHILE OTHERS ARE MORE LIKELY TO DEPRECIATE.
THE WINNER OF THIS CHALLENGE WILL BE GIVEN THE FIRST CHOICE OF WHICH ASSETS HE OR SHE WILL INHERIT.
SO THAT MEANS THE DIFFERENT SHARES OF THE FORTUNE COULD END UP BEING EXPONENTIALLY DIFFERENT IN WORTH IN THE FUTURE.
I'VE NEVER ASKED MY FATHER-IN-LAW FOR HELP RUNNING MY COMPANY.
AND I'M NOT COUNTING ON GETTING ANYTHING FROM HIM.
BUT MY WIFE DOESN'T WANT TO SIT BACK AND LET HER BROTHERS GET ALL THE PROFIT.
SHE'S FEELING A LOT OF PRESSURE.
AND AS THE JUDGE FOR THIS ASSIGNMENT...

...CHAIR-MAN OTO-NASHI HAS CHOSEN THE YOUNG IWANAGA HEIRESS.
SHE WILL EVALUATE OUR PER-FORMANCE AND DECIDE WHO BEST FULFILLED THE REQUIRE-MENTS.
BUT THAT'S CRAZY.
NONE OF THE HEIRS KNOW THE FIRST THING ABOUT THIS GIRL. WHY WOULD HE CHOOSE HER FOR SOME-THING SO IMPORTANT?
I DON'T KNOW.
I DON'T EVEN KNOW IF HE EVER HAD ANY DEALINGS WITH THE IWANAGA FAMILY BEFORE NOW.
BUT HE PER-SONALLY SELECTED HER.
THAT'S JUST HOW IT'S GOING TO BE. AND WE NEED A STRATEGY.

THE FINAL DECISION RESTS ON THIS KOTOKO IWANAGA. THAT'S WHY I WANTED TO FIND OUT MORE ABOUT HER TASTES AND PERSONALITY BEFOREHAND.
BUT I GUESS ALL I'VE LEARNED IS THAT CLUMSY ATTEMPTS TO OUTSMART HER WILL ONLY BACKFIRE.

COULD I WIN MYSELF A RELATIVE ADVANTAGE BY GETTING MY WIFE'S BROTHERS TO LOSE POINTS?
BY INCITING THEM TO TRY SOME-THING ON MISS IWANAGA?
BUT IF SHE SEES RIGHT THROUGH YOU,
AND EXPOSES YOU IN FRONT OF YOUR BROTHERS-IN-LAW, DON'T YOU THINK THAT WOULD PUT A STRAIN ON YOUR FUTURE FAMILY RELATIONS?

SO I'D HAVE TO ALLOW FOR THAT POSSIBIL-ITY, TOO, HUH?
WHAT KIND OF A GIRL AM I DEALING WITH?
THAT KIND OF GIRL, IS ALL I CAN SAY.
YOU WOULDN'T HAPPEN TO STILL BE IN TOUCH WITH THE YOUNG LADY?
I NEVER KNEW HER PHONE NUMBER OR EMAIL ADDRESS, EVEN WHEN WE WENT TO SCHOOL TOGETHER.

THAT NIGHT

POOR GUY TREATED ME TO LUNCH FOR NOTHING.

I HOPE EVERYTHING WORKS OUT FOR HIM.

たっ たと たっ

SCAMPITY SCAMPER

MANABU-KUN!

WAH!

I'M HERE!

SO FROM THE SOUNDS OF THINGS, I GUESS IWANAGA-SAN REALLY ISN'T FOLLOWING ANY NORMAL LIFE PATH.
BASED ON HER HIGH SCHOOL CAREER, I DOUBT SHE *EVER* FOLLOWED A NORMAL PATH.
I KNOW THIS IS ANCIENT HISTORY, BUT SHE *MUST* HAVE BEEN PULLING STRINGS.
YEAH, IT'S ANCIENT HISTORY, BUT I'D HAVE A HARDER TIME BELIEVING SHE WASN'T.
BUT DO YOU THINK IWANAGA-SAN WILL BE OKAY?
I'D LIKE TO THINK THE HOTEL CEO REALLY DID JUST WANT HER TO BE JUDGE, BUT IT SOUNDS LIKE HE HAD SOMETHING ELSE IN MIND.
NO MATTER HOW FAIR THE JUDGING IS, SOMEONE IS GOING TO BE UNHAPPY ABOUT IT, AND THEY'RE NOT JUST GOING TO SIT AND TAKE IT.
SO WHEN CHOOSING A JUDGE, YOU'RE GOING TO WANT SOMEONE WHO WILL GIVE A VERDICT THAT EVERYONE WILL HAVE TO ACCEPT.
IWANAGA-SAN IS DEFINITELY NOT THE RIGHT CHOICE FOR THAT.

SO I CAN'T HELP THINKING THAT CHAIRMAN OTONASHI IS ACTIVELY TRYING TO START A DISPUTE.
BUT HE'S STILL THE ONE I'M MOST WORRIED ABOUT.
THERE'S NO WAY HE CAN CONTROL IWANAGA-SAN, AND IF HE'S ACTING WITH ANY SPITE OR ULTERIOR MOTIVES, HE'S BOUND TO GET HURT.
OH!
THAT'S SOME-THING I CAN PICTURE.
I DON'T THINK THERE'S ANYONE ALIVE WHO CAN OUT-SMART HER.
IF THERE IS, THEY'D HAVE TO BE A REAL WEIRDO WHO'S DEVIATED PRETTY FAR FROM NORMAL HUMAN STANDARDS.
FLASH

WHEN ULTRAMAN DOES HIS SPECIUM RAY...
IS IT RIGHT HAND UP, LEFT TO THE SIDE?
OR THE RIGHT HAND TO THE SIDE, LEFT HAND UP?
I CAN'T REMEMBER.
BWOFF
COME TO THINK OF IT, I WONDER IF CHAIRMAN OTONASHI IS DOING HIS JOB.

CINEMAS

DO YOU THINK IWANAGA-SAN IS STILL DATING THE MAN SHE WAS CHASING ALL THOSE YEARS?

POSTER: THE ZOMBIE DETECTIVE

Purchase Tickets

ピ
BEEP

IF SHE IS, IT'S EITHER A MIRACLE, OR THERE'S SOMETHING SERIOUSLY WRONG WITH HIM.

YOU WOULD SAY THAT OUT LOUD?

THAT'S A STUPID THING TO ASPIRE TO. AND THEY'D TURN YOU DOWN AS SOON AS YOU ORDERED.
Want some popcorn?
Yeah.
OR DID YOU FORGET THAT THEY JUST TRIED TO STOP YOU FROM GOING IN TO SEE AN R-RATED MOVIE?
THEY WERE EVEN GIVING *ME* DIRTY LOOKS.

THAT'S BIG TALK FROM THE MAN WHO PRETENDED HE DIDN'T KNOW ME.
With caramel?
Sure.
I *DON'T* KNOW YOU, STRANGER.

YOU WOULD CALL ME A STRANGER WHEN YOU KNOW THAT THE UNDER-GARMENTS I AM WEARING TODAY...
...ARE PAISLEY!

WHACK
I TOLD YOU NOT TO BROAD-CAST THOSE THINGS!
OW! OW! OW!

GRG
ぎ!

AAAAAHH!

ぎ!! GRG
ぎ!! GRG
ぎ!! GRG
ぎ!! GRG
GRG ぎ!

GNG ぐ
GNG ぐ
GNG ぐ
GNG ぐ

WHOOSH
ばっ!!

WHAM
GRRRR!
WHAM

...WELL, THEY *DO* SEEM TO BE GETTING ALONG.

WANNA PRETEND WE DIDN'T SEE THAT?

PAISLEY UNDERWEAR..?

STILL, IWANAGA-SAN ALWAYS HAD SUCH A POKER FACE.

TO THINK SHE COULD BE SO EXPRESSIVE.

LANTERNS: YAKITORI, TORINIKU

THERE WAS A COUPLE BACK THERE WHO LOOKED AT US LIKE THEY'D JUST SEEN A GHOST. ANY IDEAS WHAT THAT WAS ABOUT?

Izakaya 里丸 Satomaru

SIGN: SATOMARU

BUT EVEN SO,
THEY SURE LOOKED SPEECHLESS WHEN THEY SAW US.
ANYONE WOULD BE AT A LOSS FOR WORDS AT THE SIGHT OF A SWEET, LOVELY ACQUAINTANCE SUCH AS MYSELF GETTING HER FACE SCRUNCHED.
"SWEET, LOVELY" PEOPLE DON'T BROADCAST THEIR UNDER-WEAR PATTERNS TO THE ENTIRE WORLD.
WELL, THE IMPORTANT THING IS THAT THEY'RE STILL TOGETHER.
GLUG
CHUG
CHUG
PHEW!
BUT *MORE* IMPOR-TANTLY...
WE NEED TO TALK ABOUT THIS JOB THAT CHAIRMAN OTONASHI HAS FOISTED ON ME.
WHAM

I GOT PERMISSION FOR YOU TO COME WITH ME.
BECAUSE I THINK THIS IS GOING TO BE A BIT OF A CHORE.
AND I'M GOING TO WANT YOUR HELP, KURÔ-SENPAI.

IN/SPECTRE

I've also always wanted to tie a necktie around my head, bring sushi home in a doggy bag, and walk with the unsteady gait of a drunkard as I snuggle coquettishly up to a man and say, "We missed the last train...♡"
You have too many demands.

CHAPTER 25: "SLEEPING MURDER PART 1"

CLACK
ONE DAY IN EARLY AU-GUST
CLACK
CLACK

WE'VE BEEN EXPECTING YOU, IWANAGA-SAMA.
THIS WAY, PLEASE.
I DON'T SEE ANY GUESTS. DID HE RESERVE THE WHOLE PLACE...
... JUST FOR US?
COUGH
COUGH
COUGH

HELLO, IT'S A PLEASURE TO MEET YOU.
I AM GÔICHI OTONASHI.
GÔICHI OTONASHI (81)

I DO APOLOGIZE, KOTOKO-SAN.
I'M SURE YOU WERE SURPRISED WHEN THIS OLD MAN YOU'VE NEVER MET REQUESTED AN AUDIENCE WITH YOU OUT OF THE BLUE.
BUT I COULDN'T HELP FEELING THAT YOU ARE THE ONLY ONE WHO CAN HELP ME IN THIS MATTER.
GÔICHI OTO-NASHI.
THE CHAIRMAN AND CEO OF THE FAMOUS OTONASHI GROUP, WHICH MANAGES OVER 200 HOTELS IN AND OUT OF THE COUNTRY AND IS ALSO PROMINENT IN THE REAL ESTATE AND TOURISM INDUSTRIES.
WHAT WOULD HE WANT WITH ME?

SUR-PRISE IS ONE WORD FOR IT.
BUT I'D SAY I FELT MORE... INCONVENIENCED IN THE EXTREME.
CLINK
SEEING AS THE OTONASHI GROUP HAS A RATHER LARGE INFLUENCE IN POLITICAL ARENAS, MY PARENTS COULDN'T SIMPLY BRUSH ASIDE A REQUEST FROM ITS CEO, AFTER ALL.
AND SINCE YOU SO POLITELY WENT THROUGH THEM TO MAKE YOUR INVITATION, I HAD NO CHOICE BUT TO ATTEND THIS INTERVIEW.
SSSIP
I ONLY MEANT TO ASK THEM WITH THE UTMOST COURTESY. BUT THAT CAN COME ACROSS AS INTIMIDATION WHEN YOU FIND YOURSELF IN A POSITION OF POWER.
COUGH

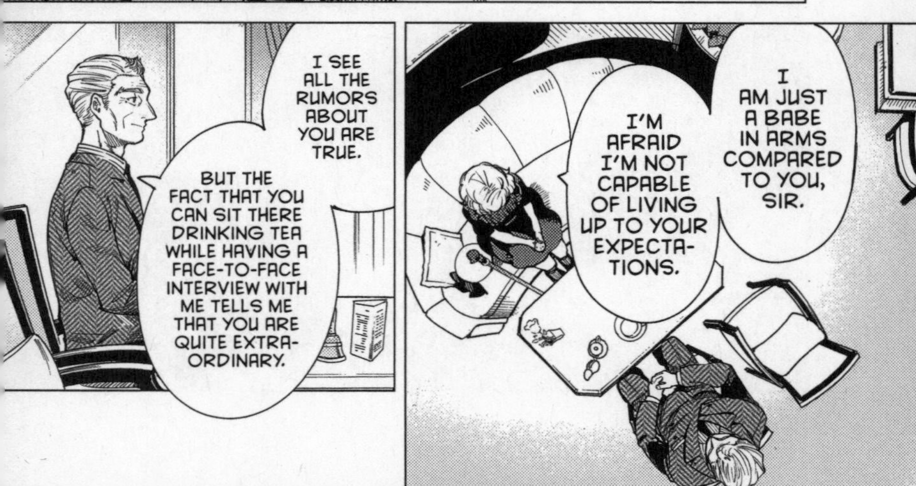

OF COURSE, PEOPLE MAY RECOGNIZE ME AS CHAIRMAN OF THE OTONASHI GROUP,
BUT I NEVER ACTIVELY SOUGHT THE POSITION.

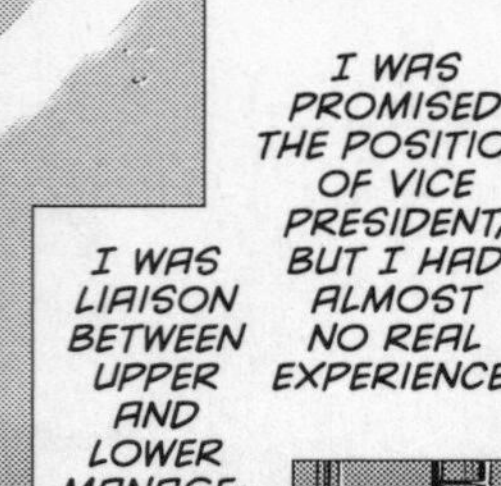

SHE WAS NAMED THE NEXT COMPANY PRESIDENT, AND I WAS THE PERFECT CHOICE TO WORK AS HER ASSISTANT.

I WAS PROMISED THE POSITION OF VICE PRESIDENT, BUT I HAD ALMOST NO REAL EXPERIENCE.

I WAS LIAISON BETWEEN UPPER AND LOWER MANAGEMENT.

OTONASHI HOTEL GROUP

SUMI-SAN DID HAVE THE BEST BUSINESS MIND OF THE TIME—SHE WAS HEAD AND SHOULDERS ABOVE THE REST.

AFTER WE GOT MARRIED, DENJIRÔ PASSED AWAY, AND SUMI-SAN BECAME THE OFFICIAL PRESIDENT, CARRYING ON IN HER FATHER'S FOOTSTEPS.

SHE EXPANDED THE COMPANY AND EVEN TURNED IT INTO A GLOBAL OPERATION.

AND ON TOP OF THAT, SHE MANAGED TO GIVE BIRTH TO THREE CHILDREN. I CAN ONLY DESCRIBE HER AS A TRUE HERO.

SHE'S NOT THE ONLY HERO—I HEARD THAT YOU'RE THE ONE WHO KEPT THE GROUP ALIVE AFTER SUMI-SAN'S PASSING.
AND THAT IF IT HADN'T BEEN FOR YOU, THE COMPANY WOULD HAVE FALLEN APART.
YES, SOME PEOPLE DO HAVE THAT OPINION.
AND PERHAPS YOU'VE HEARD THIS OPINION AS WELL?
THE GROUP WOULD HAVE GONE OUT OF BUSINESS IF SUMI-SAN HAD LIVED ANOTHER YEAR.
Stabbed to Death by Mugger
Oto-
nas
Gro
Pres
dent
Mur-
dered
President Sumi Otonashi
MBUN
YOUR WIFE WAS STABBED 23 YEARS AGO, CORRECT? THEY BELIEVE IT WAS A MUGGING?
AND THE KILLER WAS NEVER CAUGHT.

YES.
IN FACT, THAT KILLER WAS ME.
SLIP
YOU'RE JOKING.
PASH
AAHH.

I KNEW THIS WAS GOING TO BE A CHORE.
WELL, IT DOESN'T BOTHER ME THAT YOU KILLED HER.
THE MURDER HAPPENED 23 YEARS AGO. THE LAW HAS BEEN CHANGED A FEW TIMES, BUT YOU'RE STILL JUST BARELY PAST THE STATUTE OF LIMITATIONS.
BUT IF THE CASE WERE JUST A TAD FRESHER, YOU WOULD STILL BE SUBJECT TO THE LAW.

THIS ISN'T A JOKE.
OF COURSE, IT'S NOT AS IF I KILLED SUMI-SAN *PERSONALLY.*
THEN YOU HIRED SOMEONE TO DO THE DEED?

THAT WOULD MAKE MATTERS SIMPLER.
BUT IT'S NOT SO EASY TO FIND SOMEONE WHO WOULD BE WILLING TO KILL FOR YOU.
TRUE. THIS ISN'T A MOVIE OR A NOVEL.
QUITE SO.

SUMI-SAN WAS KILLED...
...BY A DEMON FOX.
SOME-THING CALLED A YÔKO.
I MADE A DEAL WITH A BEING THAT LIVES OUTSIDE THE KNOWN LAWS OF NATURE, AND IT KILLED SUMI-SAN FOR ME.
...NOW YOU'RE TAKING THIS JOKE TOO FAR.
THE CEO OF AN INTERNATIONAL HOTEL CHAIN, SPEAKING OF SUCH UNSCIEN-TIFIC THINGS AS DEMON FOXES.
IT'S *BECAUSE* I'M THE CEO OF A HOTEL CHAIN.

COUNTLESS PEOPLE PASS THROUGH HOTELS EVERY DAY. AND AS SUCH, THEY OFTEN BECOME THE SETTING FOR ALL MANNER OF HUMAN MISERY—MURDER, SUICIDE, FIRE, AND SO ON.
THAT MAY BE WHY YOU HEAR SO MANY STORIES OF GHOSTS AND OTHER PARANORMAL PHENOMENA MANIFESTING IN HOTEL ROOMS.
WHEN YOU RUN MULTIPLE HOTELS, WHETHER YOU LIKE IT OR NOT, YOU HEAR ABOUT THINGS THAT CANNOT BE EXPLAINED BY KNOWN SCIENCE.
I'LL NEVER ADMIT IT PUBLICLY...
...BUT SOME OF THOSE THINGS ARE REAL.
I DID MAKE A DEAL WITH A YÔKO 23 YEARS AGO.
WHY WOULD YOU TELL ME ABOUT THIS?

YOU'RE FAMOUS IN CERTAIN CIRCLES, AREN'T YOU?
FOR HAVING CERTAIN VIEWS ON THE SUBJECT OF SUPER-NATURAL CREATURES.

IN FACT, I'VE HEARD THAT ONE OF OUR HOTELS HAD A PROBLEM WITH SPIRITUAL PHENOMENA IN ONE OF THE GUESTROOMS, AND THE RUMORS THEY HEARD LED THEM TO SEEK YOU OUT FOR HELP.
YOU VISITED THE ROOM IN QUESTION AND SOLVED THE ISSUE RIGHT THEN AND THERE.
I DON'T THINK THERE'S ANY WAY YOU CAN DENY THAT YOU HAVE STRANGE POWERS.

IT'S TRUE THAT I SOMETIMES GET THOSE REQUESTS THROUGH MY PARENTS, AND I AM FORCED TO RELUCTANTLY COMPLY.
BUT EVERY ONE OF THOSE MATTERS COULD BE EXPLAINED LOGICALLY—BY HALLUCINATIONS, RARE NATURAL PHENOMENA, PSYCHOLOGICAL BIAS, ETC.
AND THOSE ARE THE TYPES OF EXPLANA-TIONS I ALWAYS PROVIDE.

I AM A CHILD OF SCIENCE!
MY FALSE EYE AND PROSTHETIC LEG ARE THE FRUITS OF THAT SCIENCE, AFTER ALL.

BUT YOU WOULDN'T NEED THAT FALSE EYE OR PROSTHETIC LEG IF NOT FOR THE PHENOMENON WE CALL SPIRITING AWAY.
I SEE EVIDENCE THAT YOU HAVE BEEN BLESSED BY THE SUPERNATURAL.

REGARDLESS OF WHAT YOU TELL OTHERS, I CAME TO YOU WITH THIS REQUEST BECAUSE I KNEW YOU WERE THE ONLY ONE WHO WOULD BELIEVE ME.

FORGIVE MY RUDENESS.
PLEASE CONTINUE.

23 YEARS AGO...
THE COMPANY KEPT EXPANSION AS ITS MAIN FOCUS.
"I WILL MAKE OUR HOTELS THE BEST IN THE WORLD."
THAT WAS WHAT DENJIRÔ WANTED, AND IT WAS SUMI-SAN'S GOAL.
BUT THERE WAS NO STOPPING SUMI-SAN.
BUT ALL THINGS HAVE THEIR LIMITS.
IF YOU STRETCH YOURSELF BEYOND YOUR ABILITIES, YOU REACH THE IMPOSSIBLE AND EVERYTHING CRUMBLES.
OUR COMPANY WAS GETTING CLOSER AND CLOSER TO THAT POINT.

MANY OF THE COMPANY EXECUTIVES HARBORED THE SAME MISGIVINGS, BUT NO ONE COULD STOP SUMI-SAN.

MYSELF INCLUDED.

AFTER ALL, I WAS JUST THE HUSBAND HER FATHER HAD CHOSEN FOR HER.

OUR OLDEST WANTED TO BE A CHEF, BUT SHE WOULDN'T ALLOW IT. SHE WANTED HIM TO BE HER SUCCESSOR.

SHE DIDN'T APPROVE OF OUR DAUGHTER'S BOYFRIEND, SO SHE TRIED TO BREAK THEM UP.

OUR YOUNGEST ACTIVELY TRIED TO TAKE CERTAIN POSITIONS WITHIN THE COMPANY, BUT SHE INSISTED THE OLDEST WOULD BE THE HEIR, AND WOULDN'T GIVE HIM THE JOBS HE WANTED.

OUR CHILDREN WERE ALL CAPABLE ENOUGH TO LIVE THE LIVES THEY WANTED.

BUT SUMI-SAN WOULDN'T LISTEN. SHE WANTED TO HAVE EVERYTHING HER OWN WAY.

MOM, WAIT!

CLACK

I DOUBT SHE WAS EVEN CAPABLE OF QUESTIONING HER OWN DECISIONS.
DID YOU THREATEN HIM?
DID YOU TELL HIM YOU WOULD RUIN HIS COMPANY IF HE DIDN'T BREAK UP WITH ME?
THAT MAN ISN'T GOOD ENOUGH FOR YOU.
THERE ARE ANY NUMBER OF MEN FROM FAMILIES WORTHIER OF THE OTONASHI NAME.
I'LL SEND YOU SOME FILES LATER. YOU CAN CHOOSE ANY ONE OF THEM YOU LIKE.
NO.
I...

I WAS AT MY BREAKING POINT.
I KNEW IT WAS TRUE, BUT I DIDN'T KNOW WHAT TO DO ABOUT IT.
IF I LET THINGS STAND, SHE WOULD DESTROY OUR CHILDREN, SHE WOULD DESTROY OUR COMPANY.
THAT'S WHEN I SECLUDED MYSELF IN ONE OF OUR MOUNTAIN VILLAS TO THINK UP A PLAN.
ヒュオオオ
WHOOOOOSH

ZSHH
EVERY-THING WOULD BE FINE IF SUMI-SAN WERE JUST OUT OF THE PICTURE.
EVERYTHING WOULD BE FINE IF SUMI-SAN WERE JUST OUT OF THE PICTURE.
EVERY-THING WOULD BE FINE IF SUMI-SAN WERE JUST OUT OF THE PICTURE.
EVERYTHING WOULD BE FINE IF SUMI-SAN WERE JUST OUT OF THE PICTURE.
...IF SUMI-SAN WERE JUST OUT OF THE PICTURE.
Z-ZSH
Z-ZSH
THEN SHALL I GRANT YOU YOUR WISH?

TMP
TELL ME MORE. I AM A YÔKO.
MY KIND HAVE BEEN AROUND FOR AGES. I AM NOT BOUND BY THE LAWS OF YOUR WORLD.
HIS APPEARANCE FRIGHTENED ME, BUT THE REALITY OF THE COMPANY AND MY CHILDREN'S FUTURE SCARED ME MORE THAN ANY MONSTER.
AND I COULDN'T OPENLY DISCUSS THE MATTER WITH ANYONE ELSE.
CLLLENCH
...
SURELY NO ONE CAN BLAME ME FOR TALKING TO A FOX.
I...
I...

ALL RIGHT.
!
I'LL KILL YOUR WIFE FOR YOU.
AND I'LL MAKE SURE NO ONE SUSPECTS YOU OR YOUR FAMILY.
MURMUR
IN EXCHANGE, YOU WILL GRANT A WISH FOR ME.
I HAD NO IDEA WHAT A MONSTER WOULD WANT FROM ME.
BUT AT THE TIME, I'M SURE I WOULD HAVE MADE THE DEAL EVEN IF HE'D ASKED FOR MY LIFE.

BUT THE FOX'S WISH WAS MUCH MORE PRACTICAL THAN THAT.
ヤリ
SCRITCH
ヤリ
SCRITCH
I WANT YOU TO DEVELOP THE LAND ON THE NEXT HILL OVER AND TURN IT INTO A HUMAN HABITATION.
A RIVAL FOX CLAN HAS MOVED IN OVER THERE, AND THEY'RE GETTING STRONGER.
I WANT TO REIN THEM IN.
IF HUMANS TAKE OVER THEIR LAND, THEY'LL BE CHASED OUT AND THAT WILL LIMIT THEIR INFLUENCE.
WHAT DO YOU SAY?
I'M SURE WE CAN GET THAT LAND, AND I DON'T THINK IT WOULD BE HARD TO DEVELOP.
I CAN'T MAKE THAT CALL WITH SUMI-SAN IN CHARGE, BUT WITH HER GONE,
IT'S A POSSIBILITY.
I CAN DO IT.

IF SUMI-SAN DIES, I WILL GRANT YOUR WISH.
I WAS PREPARED TO OFFER HIM MY LIFE, SO THIS WAS A SMALL PRICE TO PAY.
THEN SHE WILL BE DEAD WITHIN THE MONTH.
ヒュオー
WHOOOOSH
ZSH
I THINK IT WAS ABOUT TEN DAYS LATER THAT SUMI-SAN WAS STABBED BY A MAN PEOPLE COULD ONLY ASSUME WAS A MUGGER.

Mugger
AND AFTER THE FUNERAL, WHEN THE COMPANY CHAOS WAS SUBSIDING...
WHRRR
CLACK
CLACK

I KILLED YOUR WIFE FOR YOU.
DON'T FORGET YOUR PROMISE.
IF YOU DON'T MAKE GOOD, YOU'RE NEXT.

YES. IT TOOK ABOUT HALF A YEAR, BUT I DEVELOPED THAT MOUNTAIN.

NO FOX CAN LIVE THERE NOW.

NOT EVERYONE WAS HAPPY WITH ME STEPPING IN AS TEMPORARY PRESIDENT.
...
BUT SOON, THE ENTIRE COUNTRY FACED AN ECONOMIC DOWNTURN.
OTHER BUSINESSES THAT HAD BEEN ON THE EXPANSION TRACK FELL LIKE DOMINOES,
PROVING THAT I WAS RIGHT TO STOP OUR EXPANSION WHEN I DID.
AFTER THAT, THE OTONASHI GROUP FOCUSED LESS ON EXPANDING, AND INSTEAD STROVE TO KEEP ITS GOALS WITHIN REASONABLE BOUNDS.
WE EVEN DOWNSIZED SOME DEPARTMENTS AND SOLD OFF OTHERS.
OTONASHI
OTEL GROUP

IF WE HAD CONTINUED ON THE COURSE SUMI-SAN HAD SET, THE OTONASHI GROUP WOULD HAVE SUFFERED A CRIPPLING BLOW.

AND WHAT HAPPENED TO YOUR CHILDREN, NOW THAT SHE WAS NO LONGER THERE TO CONTROL THEM?
I TOLD THEM THEY WERE ALL FREE TO LIVE THEIR OWN LIVES.

MY OLDEST LEFT THE FAMILY BUSINESS AND BECAME A CHEF. NOW HE RUNS HIS OWN RESTAURANT.
MY DAUGHTER MARRIED HER BOYFRIEND. HE HAS HIS OWN SUCCESSFUL BUSINESS, AND THEY'RE HAPPILY MARRIED TO THIS DAY.
AND MY YOUNGEST MADE IT INTO THE COMPANY'S ADMINISTRATIVE LEVELS, AND NOW HE'S OUR EXECU-TIVE DIRECTOR. I COULDN'T ASK FOR ANYTHING BETTER.

IN OTHER WORDS, YOUR WIFE'S PASSING REALLY DID MAKE A WONDERFUL LIFE FOR ALL OF YOU.
YES.
I MADE MY OWN LIFE'S PATH A SUCCESSFUL ONE BY VIOLATING THE TABOO OF MURDER.
IT'S SURPRISING HOW WELL THINGS HAVE GONE.

YOU KNOW THAT I'VE STEPPED DOWN FROM RUNNING THE COMPANY FOR HEALTH REASONS.

THE TRUTH IS, SEVERAL MALIGNANT TUMORS HAVE SPREAD THROUGH-OUT MY BODY, AND THE DOCTORS HAVE GIVEN ME ONE YEAR TO LIVE.

IN ABOUT HALF THAT TIME, I WILL START HAVING DIFFICULTY WALKING, I WILL SUFFER INTENSE PAIN, AND I WILL MEET A CRUEL END.

I HAVEN'T TOLD MY FAMILY ANY OF THIS YET. I'D LIKE TO KEEP IT A SECRET FOR THE TIME BEING.

BUT THAT ASIDE, I WAS ACTUALLY RELIEVED TO HEAR MY PROGNOSIS.

I FELT LIKE I'M FINALLY BEING PUNISHED FOR MY CRIME.

WITHOUT A SHADOW OF A DOUBT,
I COMMITTED MURDER.
I DESERVE TO BE PUNISHED.
ANYTHING ELSE WOULD GO AGAINST THE NATURAL ORDER.
I'VE REFUSED ANY TERMINAL CARE OR ASSISTED DEATH, AND I INTEND TO GIVE MYSELF FULLY TO THE PAIN.
I AGREE THAT IT DEFIES ORDER.
コト
CLUNK
BUT WHAT DO YOU WANT *ME* TO DO?
MY ONE CONCERN IS MY CHILDREN.
THEIR HAPPY LIVES ARE ESSENTIALLY THE RESULT OF THEIR MOTHER'S DEATH.
IT'S DANGEROUS TO EXPERIENCE SUCCESS IN THIS WAY.

IF A TIME COMES WHEN THEY COULD BENEFIT SIMILARLY FROM ANOTHER'S DEATH,
IT'S POSSIBLE THAT MURDER WILL BE THE FIRST OPTION THAT COMES TO MIND.
THIS IS WHY I MUST MAKE IT VERY CLEAR TO THEM...
...THAT I KILLED SUMI-SAN, AND I AM SUFFERING A PAINFUL DEATH AS PUNISHMENT.
BUT...
...I USED THE HELP OF A DEMON FOX TO KILL HER.
BECAUSE OF THAT, I HAVE A ROCK-HARD ALIBI. I COULDN'T POSSIBLY HAVE COMMITTED THE CRIME.
I COULD TELL THEM THE TRUTH—THAT I HAD HELP FROM A YÔKO—BUT I DOUBT MY CHILDREN WOULD BELIEVE ME.
I DON'T THINK THEY'D BELIEVE I HIRED ANYONE, EITHER.

I CAN'T PROVE MY GUILT, BECAUSE THE ONE WHO ACTUALLY COMMITTED THE CRIME WAS A FOX SPIRIT.

YES, IT WOULD BE DIFFICULT TO CONVINCE PEOPLE OF THAT.

AND SO, I MUST FIND SOME WAY TO MAKE MY CHILDREN BELIEVE THAT I AM THE ONE WHO KILLED THEIR MOTHER—

TO PROVE THAT MY IMPOSSIBLE CRIME WAS ACTUALLY POSSIBLE.

AND I WANT YOUR HELP.

EVEN IF IT MEANS LYING TO THEM ABOUT HOW THE MURDER TOOK PLACE?

YOU DON'T THINK IT WOULD SOUND MORE LIKE A LIE TO TELL THEM I MADE A DEAL WITH A FOX?

COUGH

OUR CHILDREN HAVE A RIGHT TO KNOW WHO KILLED THEIR MOTHER.

STAYING IN THE DARK WOULD BE LIKE HAVING A THORN PERMANENTLY STUCK IN THEIR HEARTS.

I WANT TO REMOVE THOSE THORNS.

THAT'S A FAIR POINT— THE CASE NEVER WAS SOLVED.

I'M SURE IT DOES BOTHER THEM OCCASIONALLY.

I HAVE COME UP WITH A DETAILED PLAN...

...TO CONVINCE THEM OF MY GUILT, AND I ALREADY HAVE A ROLE FOR YOU.

Ha ha ha.

チリン

ALING

I CAN SEE WHY EVERYONE TALKS ABOUT YOU.

I WISH I'D GOTTEN TO KNOW YOU SOONER.

AND THAT'S WHAT WE TALKED ABOUT TWO WEEKS AGO.

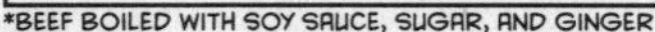
*BEEF BOILED WITH SOY SAUCE, SUGAR, AND GINGER

THUD
WE CAUGHT THE SCOUNDREL YOU WERE LOOKING FOR, MY LADY!
YES.
BASED ON THE INFORMATION I HAD, THERE WAS ONLY ONE FOX IT COULD HAVE BEEN, SO I FOUND HIM RELATIVELY QUICKLY.
GRRRRR!
RUMBLE
RUMBLE
MY NAME IS FUBUKI.
YOU ACCUSE ME, A PURE AND NOBLE YÔKO, OF ASSISTING A LOWLY HUMAN? I'VE NEVER BEEN SO INSULTED!
RELEASE ME! OR I SHALL USE MY YÔKAI POWERS TO BRING DISASTER UPON THIS LAND...

YIP! キャ
WHAP
WE ALL KNOW YOU DID IT!
YOU USED A HUMAN TO DESTROY THE MOUNTAINS! THAT'S UNFORGIV-ABLE!
EEP!
WHAP
EEEEK! HELP ME!
WE'RE LOSING ALL OUR HABITABLE LAND AS IT IS!
INNOCENT SPIRITS LOST THEIR HOMES THANKS TO YOU!
WHAP
YIP
YIP
...
WH-WHY?
HOW CAN YOU BE SO CERTAIN THAT I'M THE GUILTY PARTY?
PROOF!
WHERE'S YOUR PROOF ?!
CHAIRMAN OTONASHI CONFESSED THE WHOLE THING.
WH-WH-WH—
WHAT DID YOU SAY?!
CLAAAANG
AFTER ALL THESE YEARS, NOW HE BETRAYS ME?!

I'M SURE YOUR FELLOW YÔKO WILL HAVE THEIR OWN WAY OF DEALING WITH YOU IN REGARDS TO THIS MATTER.

BUT IF YOU STOP RESISTING AND ALLOW ME TO INTERROGATE YOU ABOUT SUMI OTONASHI'S MURDER, I CAN PUT IN A WORD TO GET THEM TO REDUCE YOUR SENTENCE.

TELL ME THE WHOLE TRUTH.

HNGH...

WHO'D'VE THOUGHT IT'D BE THE **HUMANS** WHO EXPOSED ME...

SIGH

IT'S REASONABLE TO ASSUME THAT YOU DON'T HAVE TO SPECIFICALLY ***TELL*** SOMEONE NOT TO TALK ABOUT A MURDER TO PREVENT THEM FROM SPILLING THE BEANS.

FUBUKI WAS A SLY FOX, BUT IN THE END, HE GOT TRIPPED UP BY CHAIRMAN OTONASHI'S CONSCIENCE.

YOU DON'T THINK IT WAS YOUR INFAMY IN CERTAIN SOCIAL CIRCLES THAT DEALT THE FATAL BLOW?

IF NOT FOR THAT, THE CEO WOULDN'T HAVE GONE TO YOU AT ALL.

YES, I'M SURE THOSE WHO ENVY MY SWEET LOVELINESS *WOULD* BE SPREADING BASELESS RUMORS ABOUT ME.

M
100% cotton
Rubber, 55% nylon, polyester
Made in Japan
OH, THEY'RE NOT BASELESS.
ANYWAY, I DID RUN INTO SOME SURPRISES, BUT I HEARD THE OTHER SIDE OF CHAIRMAN OTONASHI'S STORY.
STAAARE
じー

SO WHAT'S GOING TO HAPPEN TO FUBUKI?
ガラ
RATTLE

WELL, IT'S NATURAL FOR YÔKO TO DECEIVE AND USE HUMANS.
SO IT DOESN'T IMMEDIATELY GO AGAINST THE NATURAL ORDER.
EVEN IF THEY BRING REAL MISFORTUNE TO HUMANS, I DON'T NECESSARILY NEED TO JUMP IN AND TAKE THEM TO TASK.

ON THE OTHER HAND, EVEN IF PEOPLE DO HARM TO MONSTERS,
THAT DOESN'T MEAN IT REQUIRES MY IMMEDIATE ATTENTION, EITHER.

THAT'S TRUE.
IT'S NOT FAIR TO MAKE MONSTERS ABIDE BY HUMAN LAWS.
ぱた
SHUT
AND ON THE OTHER HAND, IT WOULD BE HEAVY-HANDED TO JUDGE HUMANS BY MONSTERS' STANDARDS.
ガララ
RATTLE
IF THE CLANS ARE HAVING DISPUTES AMONGST THEMSELVES, IT'S NOT MY JOB TO ARBITRATE THEM.
IT IS RIGHT AND PROPER TO LET THE FOXES DECIDE HIS FATE.
OF COURSE, IF THEY DID COME TO ME FOR ADVICE, THEN I WOULD PRONOUNCE SOME SORT OF JUDGMENT.
とん
TMP
BUT THEY TOOK FUBUKI AND MARCHED OFF WITHOUT ME.
FARE-WELL.
WE SHALL DECIDE HIS FATE, THANK YOU.

BUT CHAIRMAN OTONASHI BENEFITED FROM A PARTNER-SHIP WITH A SPECTRE.
HOW ARE YOU GOING TO DEAL WITH THAT?
DID THAT DISRUPT THE ORDER ENOUGH FOR YOU TO HAVE TO FIX IT?
Well, there is the matter of balance.
KARAOKE
カラオケ
LET'S SAY A SPIRIT SHOWS UP AT A HOTEL AND IS BOTHERING THE GUESTS AND EMPLOYEES. THEY MAY NOT LIKE IT, BUT IT'S NOT AN IMMEDIATE VIOLATION OF THE ORDER.
BUT IF IT GOES ON TOO LONG, AND THE MORTALS DECIDE TO TAKE ACTIONS AGAINST THE SUPER-NATURAL CREATURE,
THAT COULD FORCE THE SPECTRES INTO A DIFFICULT POSITION.
I TAKE STEPS TO STOP THINGS BEFORE THEY GET OUT OF HAND, IN A MANNER THAT SATISFIES BOTH PARTIES.
THAT IS MY ROLE IN ALL OF THIS.

SO GETTING A YÔKAI'S HELP TO BENEFIT YOUR BUSINESS, OR TO START A RELATIONSHIP WITH YOUR BELOVED...
OR USING *YOUR* POWERS TO GET THAT PRIZE FROM THE CLAW MACHINE...
MINOR THINGS LIKE THAT ARE ACTUALLY JUST HEART-WARMING.
I THINK THAT LAST ONE IS CHEATING.
THEN YOU MAY GET IT FOR ME WITHOUT USING YOUR POWERS.
THEY'RE JUST BALLPOINT PENS. YOU CAN BUY THEM AT THE CORNER STORE.
LOOK *CLOSER,* SENPAI.
TADAH
THESE ARE MYSTICAL PENS—THE SWIMSUIT DISAPPEARS WHEN YOU TURN THEM UPSIDE DOWN!
THE PENS YOU BUY AT THE CORNER STORE CAN'T EVEN COMPARE!
WHEN TURNED UPSIDE-DOWN, THE OPAQUE LIQUID IN THESE MYSTERIOUS PENS WILL FALL AWAY TO REVEAL A HIDDEN IMAGE UNDER THE SWIMSUITS OF THE WOMEN PICTURED.
I WANT THEM!
...
I WANT THEM!

CHA-CHING チャリーン
ANY-WAY...
WHEN IT'S A MURDER, AND ONE THAT WAS PREMEDITATED BY AN INFLUENTIAL MEMBER OF SOCIETY...
...I'M GUESSING YOU CAN'T CALL THAT "NO BIG DEAL" AND JUST LET IT HAPPEN.
CLICK カチ
THAT'S RIGHT.
AT THIS POINT, CHAIRMAN OTONASHI HASN'T TOLD ANYONE BUT ME ABOUT THIS.
HE ADMITS THAT HE COMMITTED A CRIME, AND NOW HE'S TRYING TO WARN HIS CHILDREN AGAINST IT.
KA-POP カパ
BUT THEY MIGHT THINK ABOUT IT LATER,
AND GET THE MESSAGE THAT THEY CAN TURN TO SUPERNATURAL SOURCES WHEN THEY'RE IN TROUBLE, AND THAT EVERY-THING WILL WORK OUT FOR THEM IF THEY DO.
WHRRR ウィ
WHRRR ウィ
SKFF スカ

CHAK
...I NEED TO PREVENT ANY POSSIBILITY THAT HIS CHILDREN WOULD COME AWAY WITH THAT IMPRESSION AND START TURNING TO OTHERWORLDLY POWERS FOR HELP.
AND ON THE SPECTRES' SIDE OF THINGS, IT WOULD BE WRONG TO ALLOW THEM TO ACTIVELY SEEK OUT HUMANS TO USE THEM FOR THEIR OWN ADVANTAGE.
THAT IS WHAT THE YÔKO AR PUNISHING FUBUKI FOR, AFTER ALL.
THE HUMAN INVOLVED SHOULD BE MADE TO PAY A SIMILAR PRICE.
THAT IS WHAT IT MEANS TO KEEP THE ORDER.
SKFF
BUT ISN'T CHAIRMAN OTONASHI PAYING THE PRICE ALREADY? HE DOESN'T HAVE MUCH LONGER TO LIVE.
CHA
IT *WOULD* BE A PRICE IF HE HAD FALLEN ILL WHEN HE WAS YOUNGER, BUT THE MAN IS 81.
AT THAT AGE, IT'S POSSIBLE THAT SOME-THING OTHER THAN CANCER WILL COME ALONG AND PUT HIM OUT OF HIS MISERY.

HIS ASSOCIATES MIGHT SEE THAT AND THINK THAT HE MADE THE CORRECT CHOICE AFTER ALL.
AND THE CEO WOULD PASS ON THINKING HE MAY HAVE BEEN RIGHT ALL ALONG.
I'M GOING TO NEED TO LAY SOME GROUND-WORK.

NO SELF-RESPECTING ADULT IN THE NORMAL WORLD WOULD EVER TRUST ME THIS MUCH.

IT'S A SIGN THAT, SOMEWHERE IN HIS MIND, CHAIRMAN OTONASHI THINKS IT'S RIGHT TO TURN TO THINGS THAT EXIST OUTSIDE OF NORMAL REASON WHEN HE NEEDS HELP.

THAT MEANS THAT HE HIMSELF IS HELD CAPTIVE BY THE PAST SUCCESS THAT HE PERSONALLY WON THROUGH UNEARTHLY ASSISTANCE.

ERGO, IN THIS INSTANCE, IT IS NECESSARY TO STEP IN AND FULFILL MY ROLE.

OH, SO YOU'RE SAYING NO ONE WOULD HAVE ANYTHING TO DO WITH YOU UNLESS THEY HAD A LOT OF TRUST IN THE SUPERNATURAL.

SO WHAT IS THE PLAN, SPECIFICALLY?

IT SOUNDED LIKE HE HAD AN IDEA?

BRINGING IN A COMPLETE STRANGER TO FORCE THEM TO ACCEPT THAT I AM A MURDERER STILL WON'T MAKE THEM BELIEVE IT DEEP DOWN.
SO I WILL MAKE THEM THINK UP THEIR OWN EXPLANATIONS...
...CAUSING THEM TO SUSPECT ME IN THE PROCESS.
ONCE THAT SEED IS PLANTED, ALL THEY'LL NEED IS A PLAUSIBLE THEORY, AND THEY'LL BE CONVINCED.
AND WITH THAT IN MIND, HE CALLED HIS CHILDREN...
ASSIGNMENT
"I KILLED MY WIFE SUMI-SAN 23 YEARS AGO. EXPLAIN HOW THAT IS TRUE."
...AND ASSIGNED THEM TO DO JUST THAT.
WHOEVER ACCOMPLISHES THE ASSIGNMENT BEST WILL BE GIVEN PRIORITY WHEN SPLITTING THEIR FATHER'S INHERITANCE.
AND MY JOB IS TO JUDGE THE CHILDREN'S THEORIES,
AND RANK THEM FROM BEST TO WORST.

AN AS-SIGNMENT TO GET AN INHERI-TANCE.
SOUNDS LIKE TROUBLE.

I SUSPECT CHAIRMAN OTONASHI HOPES THIS ASSIGNMENT WILL REMIND THEM OF THE MURDER.
HE WANTS THEM TO SEE IT THROUGH THAT FILTER, AND TO START QUESTION-ING EVERYTHING. THEN THEY'LL BE IN A FRAME OF MIND THAT MAKES IT EASIER FOR THEM TO BELIEVE THAT THEIR FATHER IS A MURDERER.
A murderer...?

YOU CAN MAKE SOME ENEMIES JUDGING THAT KIND OF A COM-PETITION.
YOU DON'T THINK SOME OF THEM WILL TRY TO COZY UP TO YOU AND GET YOU TO RULE IN THEIR FAVOR?
¥100 1 try
¥500 6 tries

YES, AND I'M SURE SOME OF THEM WILL SIC PRIVATE INVESTIGA-TORS ON ME.
ぱち
CLICK

BUT I WON'T ONLY BE THE JUDGE. HE ALSO EXPECTS ME TO OFFER ADVICE,
AND HELP THEM COME UP WITH THE MOST APPROPRI-ATE EXPLA-NATIONS.

HE TOLD ME TO MAKE SURE THEIR THEORIES HAD NO OBVIOUS CONTRADIC-TIONS OR MISTAKES.
AND THE PURPOSE OF THAT IS TO HELP THEM ARRIVE AT MORE ACCURATE CONCLUSIONS.
WHRRR
WHRR
ACCURATE CONCLUSIONS NOTHING. THE TRUTH IS HE GOT A FOX SPIRIT TO KILL HER, RIGHT?
THACK
Grrr!
PLOP
Umm
WHAT I MEAN IS AN AC-CURATE,
FALSE ...
...EXPLA-NATION.

HE SAYS HE HAS AN ALIBI.

IT WON'T BE EASY TO COME UP WITH A WAY TO EXPLAIN HOW THEIR FATHER WAS THE MURDERER.

THE CEO THINKS HIGHLY OF HIS CHILDREN'S TALENTS, BUT I'M NOT SO SURE.

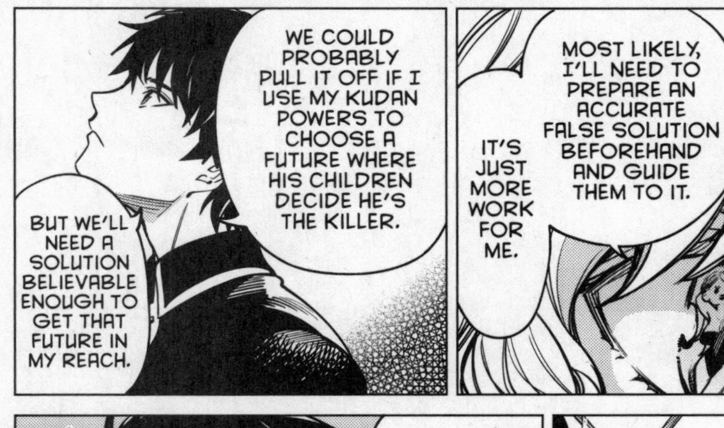

I ASKED HIM THE SAME QUESTION, BUT...
WITH AN OUTSIDER PRESENT, MY CHILDREN WILL BE FORCED TO BELIEVE THAT THIS ISN'T JUST SOME JOKE.
AND SINCE YOU BELIEVE IN SPECTRES, YOU BELIEVE THAT I KILLED SUMI-SAN.
KNOWING A THIRD PARTY THINKS I'M GUILTY WILL STRENGTHEN THE IDEA IN THEIR MINDS THAT WHAT I CLAIM IS ACTUALLY TRUE.
AND THAT'S WHAT HE SAID.
HE'S JUST BOUND AND DETERMINED TO USE ME FOR HIS OWN GAIN.
P-LOP
1 TRY LEFT
Your turn, senpai.
HUFF
HUFF
don't think anybody can get it now!

THE CHILDREN'S REPRESENTATIVES ARE TO GATHER AT THE HOTEL AT NOON ON SEPTEMBER 3 TO PRESENT THEIR SOLUTIONS.
BUT WE WON'T HEAR THEIR FINAL ANSWERS UNTIL NOON THE FOLLOWING SUNDAY.
IN THE MEANTIME, THE REPRESENTATIVES AND I WILL DEBATE, EXCHANGE INFORMATION, AND REVISE THEIR ANSWERS.
WHRR
WOW, THAT SOUNDS LIKE TORTURE.
WHRR
YOU'RE GOING TO BE THERE, TOO, KURÔ-SENPAI.
I THINK I HAVE WORK THIS WEEKEND.
SO TELL THEM YOU CAN'T GO IN.
ARE YOU TRYING TO SEND ME INTO THAT HORRIBLE GATHERING BY MYSELF?
I HAVE NO CHOICE.
I'LL JUST HAVE TO GIVE SENPAI SOME INCENTIVE.
zero motivation

I DO FEEL BAD FOR DRAGGING YOU INTO THIS.
WHICH IS WHY I WORE SEXY UNDERWEAR TODAY, JUST FOR YOU.
す
SFF

BELIEVE IT OR NOT, IT HAS A **PAISLEY PATTERN.** JUST SEE FOR YOURSELF.
PEEK
ちら

STOP THAT!
ばっ
WHOOSH

YOU HAVE ZERO SEX APPEAL TO BEGIN WITH.
AND ZERO TIMES ANY-THING WILL ALWAYS BE ZERO.
NOT TO MENTION, PAISLEY IS THE OPPO-SITE OF SEXY.
WHAT! YOU MEAN TO TELL ME YOU DON'T UNDERSTAND ITS RAUNCHY CHARM?!
だん
BAM

WHRR
ウィィ
ウィィ
WHRR
ポフ
THUNK

WE DID IT!
POING
ぴょん
YOU GOT IT, SENPAI!
POING
ぴょん

ちゅばばば
MWAH
MWAH
MWAH
MWAH
IT FEELS GOOD TO GET A PRIZE, NO MATTER WHAT IT IS.

PICK UP
I'LL BE THERE ON SATURDAY.

BUT I THINK DEALING WITH THESE MORTALS IS GOING TO BE MORE EXHAUSTING THAN ANY YÔKAI OR MONSTER PROBLEM YOU'VE HAD TO SOLVE.

SPARKLE
SPARKLE
AGREED.
BUT I HAVE A PLAN, SO YOU HAVE NOTHING TO WORRY ABOUT.
IT'S JUST ...

JUST WHAT?

NEVER MIND.
IT'S NOTH-ING.

HOW IS THIS CEO SO SURE THAT HE CAN TRUST ME TO DO ALL THIS?
THAT'S THE ONE THING THAT STILL BOTHERS ME...
OH!

—SEPTEMBER 3 (SATURDAY)—

1517
AS I ASKED YOU ALL BEFORE ...
AHEM
...I WOULD LIKE YOU TO PRESENT LOGICAL EXPLANATIONS AS TO HOW I KILLED SUMI OTONASHI-SAN.

WHOEVER PROVIDES THE BEST ANSWER WILL BE GIVEN PRIORITY WHEN I DIVIDE MY FORTUNE FOR YOUR INHERI-TANCE.
KOTOKO IWANAGA-SAN HAS JOINED US TO EVALUATE YOUR THEORIES.
UNTIL THEN, YOU MAY SUBMIT AS MANY EXPLANATIONS TO KOTOKO-SAN AS YOU LIKE.
YOU MAY ALSO ALTER AND REVISE YOUR ANSWERS.
I WILL RETURN TOMORROW AT NOON TO HEAR YOUR FINAL ANSWERS.

KOTOKO-SAN WILL DECIDE THE RESULTS BASED ON YOUR FINAL ANSWERS TOMORROW.

IN THE MEANTIME, SHE WILL HEAR YOUR THEORIES AND QUESTIONS, AND SUPPLY CRITIQUE AND ADVICE AS REQUIRED.

HE CALLS ALL THESE PEOPLE INTO ONE PLACE TO FIGHT OVER THE INHERITANCE.

IT'S LIKE HE'S INTENTIONALLY SETTING THE STAGE FOR A MURDER.

AND APPARENTLY HE JUST CAN'T WAIT TO BE BRANDED A KILLER.

...

MY YOUNGEST SON SUSUMU.

SUSUMU OTONASHI (50)

THE EXECUTIVE DIRECTOR OF THE OTONASHI GROUP.

KAORUKO'S HUSBAND, KÔYA FUJINUMA-KUN.

THE PRESIDENT OF HIS OWN USED CAR COMPANY.

HE HAS SHARPER WITS AND MORE GRIT THAN KAORUKO. HE WAS ALWAYS MORE LIKELY TO GIVE THE BETTER ANSWER, SO I'M NOT SURPRISED THAT HE CAME IN HIS WIFE'S PLACE.

IF KÔYA-KUN IS CONVINCED THAT I KILLED SUMI-SAN, THEN KAORUKO IS SURE TO BELIEVE HIM.

KÔYA FUJINUMA (56)

RION, DAUGHTER OF MY OLDEST, RYÔMA, AND MY GRAND-DAUGHTER.

RYÔMA HAS NEVER CARED ABOUT ANYTHING MORE THAN COOKING. HE WOULD NEVER LEAVE HIS RESTAURANT FOR THIS.

RION OTONASHI (21)

RION'S GRAND-MOTHER WAS MURDERED BEFORE SHE WAS BORN.

THIS WILL GIVE HER A NEW PERSPECTIVE, WHICH SHE CAN SHARE WITH ALL OF YOU, AS SHE WILL SEE THE CASE WITHOUT ANY PRE-CONCEPTIONS.

AND THESE ARE OUR THREE CONTEND-ERS.

DAD.

I CAME HERE BECAUSE, DESPITE ALL MY QUESTIONS, YOU NEVER GAVE ME A STRAIGHT ANSWER.

WHAT ARE YOU TRYING TO DO HERE?

EXACTLY WHAT I TOLD YOU.
I SIMPLY WANT TO TEACH YOU THE TRUTH ABOUT WHO KILLED YOUR MOTHER,
AND SHOW YOU THAT WE MUST ALWAYS FACE PUNISHMENT FOR OUR CRIMES.

BUT YOU COULDN'T HAVE KILLED MOM.
EVEN IF YOU DID, WHAT'S THE POINT IN CONDEMNING YOU FOR IT NOW?
YOU WILL KNOW EXACTLY WHAT THE POINT IS ONCE YOU HAVE ARRIVED AT THE TRUTH.

THEN WHY DID YOU CHOOSE THIS YOUNG LADY TO JUDGE THE ASSIGN-MENT?
YOU COULDN'T HAVE FOUND SOMEONE MORE UNRELATED TO THE FAMILY. IF YOU DID KILL OUR MOTHER, THAT'S ALL THE MORE REASON SHE SHOULDN'T BE HERE.

KOTOKO-SAN IS THE ONE PERSON MOST QUALIFIED TO EVALU-ATE THE TRUTH.

SFF
す,

I HAVEN'T INTRO-DUCED MYSELF.
I AM KOTOKO IWANAGA.
THE MAN STANDING BEHIND ME IS KURÔ SAKURA-GAWA.
MY RIGHT EYE IS GLASS AND MY LEFT LEG IS PROSTHETIC, SO I OBTAINED PERMISSION FOR HIM TO ACCOMPANY ME ON THE OFF-CHANCE THAT I WOULD NEED ASSISTANCE.
NEITHER I NOR SAKURAGAWA WILL DISCLOSE ANYTHING WE SEE OR HEAR IN THIS ROOM.
WHEN WE LEAVE HERE TOMORROW, I ASSURE YOU WE WILL FORGET THE ENTIRE AFFAIR.
SO YOU MAY DISCUSS THE MATTER AND PRESENT YOUR ANSWERS TO ME WITH NO FEAR FOR YOUR FAMILY'S REPUTATION.

I WILL HONOR CHAIRMAN OTON-ASHI'S WISHES...
...AND EVALUATE ALL OF YOUR THEORIES FAIRLY, ALWAYS WITH A MIND TO MAINTAIN TRUTH AND ORDER.
SFF
AND THERE YOU HAVE IT. I LOOK FORWARD TO HEARING YOUR ANSWERS TOMORROW.
NOW, ONE FINAL TIME.

◆ TO BE CONTINUED IN VOLUME 11

Please
enjoy the
anime,
too!

A Discussion of Forms of Address from the Author

I am the author, Kyo Shirodaira, and this is volume 10. We've finally made it to the double digits. In this volume, we've returned to the overarching plot, where Rikka Sakuragawa lurks in the shadows, pulling the strings. But unlike last time, this won't be a single ongoing case—rather, I think the story will unfold in a different way, until it all comes together. Everything will be connected piece by piece. ...Or not.

Now, let us speak of the detective—the main character of this series, "Kotoko Iwanaga." I generally refer to her as Iwanaga. The narrative text of the novel always calls her Iwanaga, and Kurô calls her Iwanaga, too.

On the other hand, it seems that many of the people I know, as well as many readers, call her Kotoko. She is almost never referred to as Kotoko in the story, and I don't think the name shows up very often at all, but I get the feeling that most people call her Kotoko or Kotoko-chan. I don't think she's cute enough (as a person) to earn the moniker of -chan, but maybe it happens anyway because of the strong impression left by the visuals in the manga. Even though she's already old enough to legally drink alcohol.

Of course you're welcome to call her whatever you want, and I'm not so stubborn that I would insist on calling her Iwanaga if I'm talking or writing to someone who calls her Kotoko, but ***in*** the series, the name "Iwanaga" is given priority.

There are a few different reasons for this, but one of them is that when I'm writing a story from a detective's perspective, I'm usually focused on making it hardboiled. And I have this personal idea that a hardboiled main character always goes by their surname.

IN/SPECTRE

Sam Spade is Spade, Lew Archer is Archer, and Philip Marlowe is Marlowe. Those are some famous examples, but of course I'm sure there are many examples that don't follow that rule. Even so, whenever someone goes by their last name, I always feel like they're "mature and edgy"—like they're hardboiled.

That is why I refer to the tough, unyielding Kotoko Iwanaga-san as "Iwanaga." But that's no reason everybody should have to do it, so please call her whatever the occasion demands. The famous female private detective Cordelia Gray goes by Cordelia, after all. But in a sense, maybe Cordelia is sweeter and lovelier than Iwanaga?

The Sleeping Murder arc should finish at the end of the next volume. Once again, the puzzle is based on a bizarre premise, but that won't change Iwanaga's actions. And that is exactly what will lead to a tangle of ambitions.

Well, I hope you will read the next volume.

Kyo Shirodaira

Bonus Manga: "Mountain-Climbing Revival"
I NEED YOUR HELP, SENPAI! THERE WAS A LANDSLIDE THE OTHER DAY ON MT. A.
I GOT AN SOS TELLING ME THE MANDRAKE THAT LIVED THERE IS STRANDED AT THE DISASTER SITE.
AND WHY ARE YOU DRESSED LIKE THAT?
ぎょっ
GAPE
THE DISTRESS CALL CAME WHILE I WAS GETTING READY TO SEDUCE YOU.
YOU TALK LIKE I'M SUPPOSED TO BE TURNED ON BY THAT SWIMSUIT.
My fisherman's flag swimsuit, wasted.
ANYONE WHO PULLS A MANDRAKE OUT OF THE GROUND WILL DIE.
SO NEITHER I NOR ANY SPECTRE CAN HELP.
Help!
AND SO I WOULD LIKE MY IMMORTAL SENPAI TO GO PULL UP THE MANDRAKE AND MOVE IT TO SAFETY.
MANDRAKE
A ROOT VEGETABLE SHAPED LIKE A HUMAN BEING THAT UNLEASHES A TERRIBLE SCREAM WHEN PULLED OUT OF THE GROUND. ALL WHO HEAR IT PERISH.
YOU WANT ME TO HIKE INTO THE MOUNTAINS, ALONE, TO PULL A WEED.
Nnngh
INCI-DENTALLY, I UNDERSTAND THAT WILD VEGETABLES GROW IN ABUNDANCE ON MT. A AT THIS TIME OF YEAR.
THIS IS A LOT OF WILD VEGETA-BLES.
THERE'S EVEN ALPINE LEEK.
ざっく
SHOONK
ざっく
SHOONK
HM?

IS THIS WHERE THE LANDSLIDE WAS?
ひょこ HOP
YOU MUST BE THE MANDRAKE IWANAGA TOLD ME ABOUT.
S-SUCH A HIDEOUS, UGLY, GROTESQUE MONSTER—YOU MUST BE MY LADY'S RIGHT-HAND MAN, KURÔ-DONO!
OKAY, LET'S GET YOU MOVED AND GO HOME.
OH, WHAT A KIND, FRIENDLY MANNER YOU HAVE, SO CONTRARY TO YOUR HORRIBLE APPEARANCE. THANK YOU.
THIS MIGHT HURT A LITTLE, BUT JUST BEAR WITH ME.
むんず GRAB
Rgh!
GRRG
ブチ SNAP
Rgrgh!
ブチ SNAP
Grgrgh!
TUG
スポン SPLOOMP
YEEAAARGH!!

ドッ
THUD
Ngh...
BLINK ぱち
AAAARGH!
?!

UGH, FOR CRYING OUT LOUD.
THAT WAS A LOT OF DEATH.
I HAD TO DIE WAY TOO MANY TIMES JUST TO GRAB A FUTURE WHERE TREE BRANCHES HAPPENED TO DESTROY BOTH MY EARDRUMS.
ガサ
RUSTLE
ガサ
RUSTLE
すや
zzz
すや
zzz
IT STOPPED SCREAMING WHEN I WRAPPED IT IN THIS CLOTH.
すや...
zzz
Okay.
LET'S HURRY AND GO HOME.
ガチッ
CLICK
ガシャ
CLANK
WH-WHAT? A HUNTER'S TRAP?
uh.
クポッ
BOP
AAAAGH
AAAARRGH!

I'll be safe here!
WHEW...
I DON'T KNOW HOW I DID IT, BUT YOU'RE ALL MOVED NOW.
YOU'VE SAVED ME, KURÔ-DONO!

TO THANK YOU, I'LL GIVE YOU A PART OF MY ROOT.
YOUR ROOT?

OUR ROOTS ARE FAMOUS FOR THEIR EFFICACY, WHICH IS WHY SO MANY HUMANS HAVE BEEN WILLING TO RISK DEATH TO GET THEM.
WOW, WHAT KIND OF EFFICACY?
AS AN APHRODISIAC, FOR IMPROVED HORMONE PRODUCTION, VIRILITY ENHANCEMENT, ETC. ETC.

IN OTHER WORDS, YOU CAN MAKE HORNY MEDICINE.

HORN—
NOW!
URRRGH!
SNAP
SNAP
SNAP
FORGET IT.

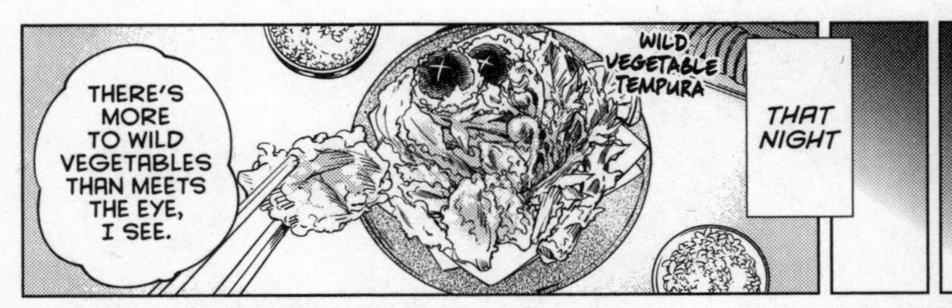

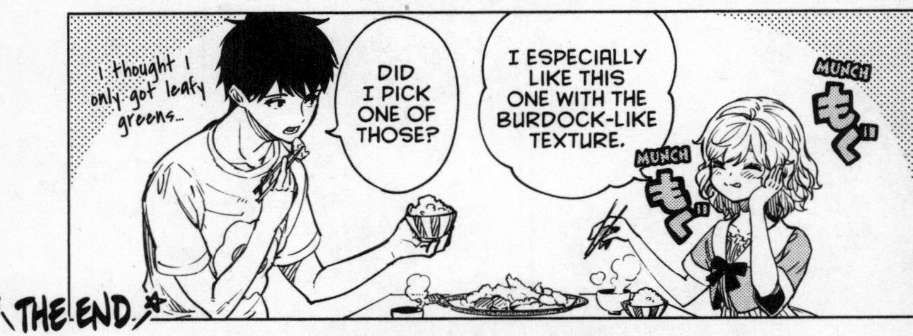

THANK YOU FOR READING VOLUME 10! I HOPE YOU'LL READ VOLUME 11, TOO!
STAFF: ASAI, SHIMAMEGURI, UMI, EDITOR: O-GAWA, T-DA

Volume
10!

TRANSLATION NOTES

Manju Kowai, page 7

Manju Kowai is a famous story from the rakugo genre of traditional Japanese entertainment. In rakugo, a single storyteller will sit before the audience and act out a story, playing all the roles him or herself. In this particular story, a group of friends sits around discussing what they hate the most or are most afraid (*kowai*) of. One of the friends reluctantly admits that he is afraid of manju—dumplings with sweet red bean filling. His "friends" then decide to play a trick on him by surprising him with dozens of manju, so they can get a kick out of seeing him run around in terror. But after they throw the manju at him and close the door, all is quiet—there is no screaming to be heard. The truth is, this man loves manju, and knew that his friends would give him a lot of them if he pretended to be scared of them. Outraged that their trick failed, his friends demand to know what he's really afraid of, to which he replies that he might be afraid of tea now. The story is from 1768, so the spoiler ban has surely been lifted for years by now.

Skeleton-woman, page 9

In the original text, Kotoko calls Rikka a *sukima onna*, or "gap-woman," referring to a Japanese urban legend about a supernatural woman who spies on people from the gaps in their apartment—such as the gap between the dresser and the wall. The point is that Rikka, like the gap-woman, is skinny and spooky. To get the insults across without slowing down the readers, the translators had Kotoko call Rikka a skeleton instead.

Seaweed wine, page 46

Seaweed wine, or *wakame zake*, is an "adult" beverage in multiple senses of the word. While it can literally mean sake with seaweed in it, in this case Kotoko is referring to a practice of having a woman kneel or sit on the floor with her knees in front of her, and using the container made by her legs and crotch to hold an alcoholic beverage. The "seaweed" is her pubic hair. This wouldn't work as well if the woman is thin enough to have a thigh gap, so girls meatier than Kotoko are more suited to the practice.

Snake with a woman's head, page 47

To be specific, Kotoko compares Rikka to a *nure-onna*, a yôkai with the body of a snake and the head of a woman. The name literally means "wet woman," and comes from the fact that they are always found near bodies of water and appear to be soaking wet. They are also known for tricking unsuspecting humans into helping them, and then sucking their blood.

Kaen Daiko, page 65

Kaen Daiko, or "Big Drum," is the rakugo tale of a poor merchant who is terrible at his job. After some twists and turns, he miraculously manages to sell a drum to a feudal lord for a significant sum of money. This experience causes him and his wife to consider what they should acquire to sell next, speculating that something else that makes noise would be similarly successful. When the merchant suggests a fire bell (a bell like the one pictured here, used as a fire alarm), his wife replies that that would be a bad idea, because *ojan ni narimasu*, which can either mean "they go 'gong,'" or "it will ruin everything."

Threw salt on myself, page 87

In Shinto, salt is used for purification. It is scattered on people and places to cast out impurities and ward of evil or unlucky spirits. Incidentally, when the girl says, "Like I was a whole new person," she uses an idiom that literally means "like whatever was possessing me fell away." This expression is used in Japan to describe situations where someone suddenly recovers either from an illness or from a bad attitude, whether or not anyone believes the person was literally possessed.

Ultraman's Specium Ray, page 117

Ultraman is a classic Japanese superhero from the 1960s. He fires a special Specium Ray by holding his right hand up vertically, and crossing his left hand horizontally in front of it.

***Yôko*, page 138**

Literally meaning "supernatural fox," a *yôko* is a fox with supernatural powers.

In/Spectre volume 10 is a work of fiction. Names, characters, places, and incidents are the products of the author's imagination or are used fictitiously. Any resemblance to actual events, locales, or persons, living or dead, is entirely coincidental.

A Kodansha Comics Trade Paperback Original.

In/Spectre volume 10 copyright © 2019 Kyo Shirodaira/Chashiba Katase
English translation copyright © 2019 Kyo Shirodaira/Chashiba Katase

All rights reserved.

Published in the United States by Kodansha Comics,
an imprint of Kodansha USA Publishing, LLC, New York.

Publication rights for this English edition arranged through Kodansha Ltd., Tokyo.

First published in Japan in 2019 by Kodansha Ltd., Tokyo, as *Kyokou Suiri* volume 10.

ISBN 978-1-63236-842-3

Printed in the United States of America.

www.kodanshacomics.com

9 8 7 6 5 4 3 2 1

Translation: Alethea Nibley & Athena Nibley
Lettering: Lys Blakeslee
Editing: Ajani Oloye
Kodansha Comics edition cover design: Phil Balsman